Oil Beneath Our Feet

America's Energy Non-Crisis

Copyright © 2009
by
David E. Robinson

MAINE-PATRIOT.com
3 Linnell Circle
Brunswick, Maine 04011

maine-patriot.com

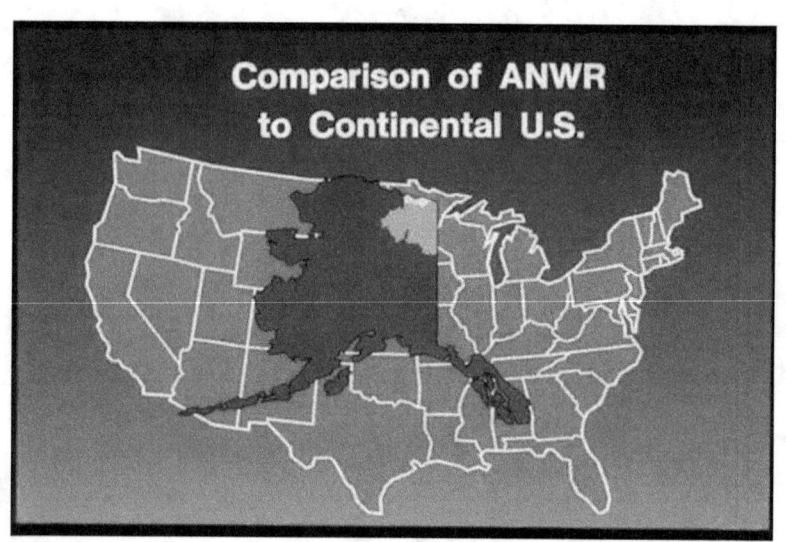

Comparison of ANWR to Continental U.S.

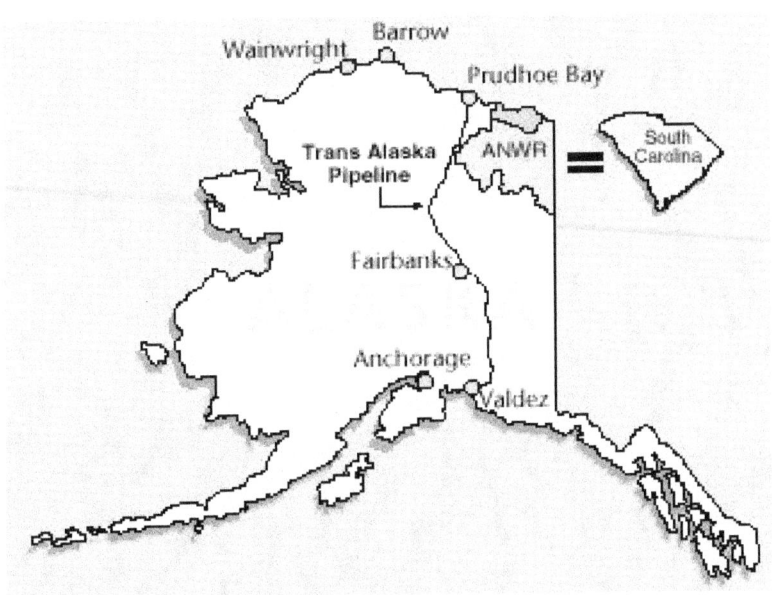

For more than 15 years drilling for oil in the **Arctic National Wildlife Refuge** (**ANWR**) has been pitched as a solution to the nation's energy needs.

A small section of ANWR, in particular along the coast known as Area 1002, has been proposed for exploration. It's is about 80 miles to the East of Prudhoe Bay, where the Trans-Alaska Pipeline System begins.

Another North Slope oil field is the **National Petroleum Reserve in Alaska (NPRA)** to the West of Prudhoe Bay.

How much oil is in ANWR? No one really knows for sure, but the latest estimate is between 5.7 and 16.0 billion barrels within Area 1002.

How much oil is in NPRA? According to the latest study, an equal amount, but you can't really tell unless you start to drill.

Oil Beneath Our Feet

Oil Beneath Our Feet
Contents

Oil Beneath Our Feet

Introduction

Contrary to what many Americans have been told, no "Energy Crisis" exists in America today. The documented evidence of three prominent Americans support this fact.

The first presentation in this book, is a transcription of a Lecture given by author Lindsey Williams, January 17, 2007, based upon his book *THE ENERGY NON-CRISIS*.

Lindsey Williams is an ordained Baptist Minister who went to Alaska in 1971 as a missionary Chaplain to the workers on the North Slope of Alaska who were building the Trans-Alaska Pipeline which runs from Prudue Bay, in the north, down across Alaska to Valdez.

Lindsey William's presentation is in nine parts.

http://tinyurl.com/y9xgzeo

The second presentation in this book, is a transcription of the non-technical parts of a Lecture given as a GOOGLE TECH TALK by Princeton, PHD Robert Bussard, November 9, 2006, revealing his ideas and the results of his work as a Co-founder and the Director of ENERGY/MATTER CONVERSION CORPORATION (EMC^2) regarding technical work that he was allowed to make public after more than a decade of silence.

Robert Bussard's presentation is in two parts.

http://tinyurl.com/y8eq8h8

Comments of a third American complete this book.

1
Alaska's North Slope Oil - Part 1

Rev. Lindsey Williams
January 17, 2007

I trust that you are aware that we are being controlled in every area of our lives; even the tooth brush that you will use tonight to brush your teeth with. Otherwise, what you're going to hear for the next few moments time, could be very disturbing to you. So, here are the facts.

There is as much crude oil on the north slope of Alaska as there is in Saudi Arabia.

The Governor of Alaska stated on the Bill Mayer TV Show, *Real Time,* on March 18, 2005: "There is potentially enough crude oil on the north slope of Alaska to supply the entire United States of America for 200 years." He's correct.

"Peak Oil" is a misnomer. It is an idea perpetuated by the powers-that-be for the purpose of deceiving the American public. Russia has just drilled some, what they call, super-deep wells to the depths of some 42,000 feet; super-deep wells which they call Cola-SG3. They have found massive amounts of oil. The world is nowhere near running out of crude oil.

Gasoline at the gas-pump could be less than one dollar and fifty cents a gallon within the next one year here in the United States of America if only our president and vice president and our Administration in Washington would be honest with the American people.

There is enough *natural gas* on the north slope of Alaska to supply the entire United States of America for over 200 years, if every other natural gas well were cut off tomorrow morning, at the projected rate of increased consumption. Every 24 hours at Prudhoe Bay Alaska on the north slope, where the large oil field is, they pump back into the ground one billion cubic feet of natural gas that comes up with the oil. I did not say 'million,' I said one 'billion' cubic feet.

They're using 48, 747 type aircraft jet engines to pump that one billion cubic feet of natural gas back into the ground every 24 hours.

Dr. Stan Montieth, the very famous radio talk show host, a very conservative individual — I've been on his program many times this past year — Dr. Stan said to me recently, "Lindsey, I'd like to prove what I have on my show, he said, Can you in some way verify the information that you are giving in your book, *THE ENERGY NON-CRISIS,* and the other things that you have to say?"

Yes, I will give you the name of an individual who right now is working for BP Oil Company (*Ed. BP = British Petroleum*) — BP bought out ARCO (*Ed. ARCO = Atlantic Richfield Corporation*), and BP & ARCO were basically the ones who produced the entire Prudhoe Bay Oil field, east and west side, ARCO on the east side, BP on the west side — I will give the name of an individual who was back there when I was there, who saw the Gull Island field "brought in" and proven.

I will not give his name now, for protection, because this man has said: If you can ever get a Congressman who will make a Congressional investigation of this... he said.... I will appear, even though it might cost me my life and my family.

When checked out by Dr. Stan, the individual said, "Everything he has written in his book is true; but in fact, he hasn't told what I know about what has happened since Dr. Lindsey left. Since Dr. Lindsey left the Prudhoe Oil Field as Chaplain we since have discovered *another* field as large as Gull Island; America has everything we need on the north slope of Alaska."

My book, *THE ENERGY NON-CRISIS,* is the only book on the face of the earth that tells of the largest oil pool in North America, possibly the largest oil pool on the face of the earth, that was discovered, brought in, tested, and proven, when I was there as a Chaplain; and today not one drop of that oil has ever been allowed to come to the American people, by order of the government of the United States of America!

Gasoline, within twelve months time, could be, at the gas pumps in California, less than one dollar and fifty cents a gallon, if only the administration in Washington would be honest with us as American people.

I'll never forget that day. I had just gone to Alaska as a missionary. It was 1970. It came out of the Alaska newspaper, "TransAlaska pipeline to be built. Twenty-five-thousand pipeliners to converge on the State of Alaska to build that 800 mile pipeline, four foot in diameter, largest pipe ever constructed on the face of the earth for the carrying of crude oil, $12 Billion dollars to be spent in three years time." Twenty-five thousand pipeliners to converge on the State of Alaska.

The first thing that came to my mind was, as a Baptist missionary, Twenty-five thousand of the most cusedest, drinkinest, orneyest folks on the face of the earth; and believe you me, that was the understatement of the year, when I arrived on the pipeline.

So I went to Alyeska Pipeline Service Company, and I said, Don't you need a Chaplain on the TransAlaska Pipeline? They said, We never had a Chaplain on any Pipeline in the world. We wouldn't know what to do with you. They said come back to see us later. Well, I did. I guess persistence paid off, because after a number of months they said, All right... We'll let you have the northern seven camps, including the big oil field at Prudhoe Bay down to Galbrith Lake in the Brooks Mountains. Go up there and see what you can do. Hold a worship service in each one of the camps once a day. The men don't know the difference. They work six weeks on, six weeks off, 12 hours on, 12 hours off. They don't know what Sunday is. And I did.

About six months later, Mr. R. H. King ... I'll never forget him ... came to me. He was a personnel relations man with Alyeska. And he said, Chaplain. We never knew what value you would be to us. He said, You're literally saving us thousands of dollars in counselling fees that we aren't having to pay. And we have just voted to give you executive status if you will accept it.

And I said to Mr. King, What does that mean? I've never been an executive on anybody's board, but the Lord's. And he said, Well, you can go any place you like, see anything that you'd like to see. We'll let you have your own vehicle, give you an executive pass, and we would like to invite you to sit in on our board meetings in an advisory capacity, in order to help the relationship between management and labor.

For the next three years time... only by the providence of God... 'cause it never could have been any other way...

I had the opportunity to sit with... live in the same dorms with... rub shoulders with... sit across the table from... the most powerful, controlling, manipulative men, on the face of this earth... the ones you only read about in books. It changed my life. I never knew such people existed. I've been a Baptist minister for 20 years. I'd had the privilege of being around honest people, and deacons, and good Christians, and all of a sudden I was thrown into the midst of those that you hear of, that control the world.

Oil Beneath Our Feet

2
Alaska's North Slope Oil - Part 2

Rev. Lindsey Williams
January 17, 2007

If someone had asked me in 1970, Lindsey Williams, Do you believe there's a group of people on the face to the earth who control the world? I would have said: Not only do I believe it... I would have said... Who are you a John Bircher? If someone had asked me in 1980, Lindsey Williams, Do you believe there's a group of people on the face of the earth, who tells the president what to do... who tells the Arabs what they're going to give them for a barrel of oil... who dictate to the world what they should do? I would have said: Not only do I believe it, I sat and listened to them talk about it.

For three years time... strictly by the providence of God... here I was a little aviation missionary, nobody knew who Lindsey Williams was, back out in the bush country of Alaska... and all of a sudden had the opportunity to sit and listen to the people that you only read about.

I remember one night, I'd been around them all night long, I couldn't believe there were such human beings on the face of the earth, I remember I went back to my dorm room, utterly exasperated about what I had seen, and I had heard that day. I lay down on my bed in utter frustration, and looked up at the ceiling and literally cried out to God. And I said... God... how can there be such dastardly people on the face of the earth that literally control the world?

Folks, there **are** people who control the world. They have an agenda. They know what they are doing. How do I know? I was there. I lived with them for three years time. I sat in their board meetings and heard what they had to say.

My book, *THE ENERGY NON-CRISIS,* is different from most books of this nature. I did not research someone else's material in order to write this book. This book is what I lived. First hand stories of the people that I rubbed shoulders with. Ones that I knew by their first names. And I was considered to be their Chaplain, and minister. Their power controls the world, and I write from first hand experience. I lived my story.

So finally after about two years of this, I decided that no one is ever going to believe a little missionary like me. If I decide to tell this story, no one would pay any attention to it. After all, how do they know that I am telling the truth? So I contacted a gentleman of great prestige. A man that I knew anyone would trust what he had to say. He writes the forward to my book, *THE ENERGY NON-CRISIS*. His name is Senator Hugh Chance, from the State of Colorado.

And I said, Hugh, I'd like you to come to Prudhoe Bay and spend a week with me. I'll make all of the arrangements with the oil company officials for you to see, talk with, have interviews with, anyone you'd like. He took me up on my offer. I made all of the arrangements. He came to Prudhoe Bay. He spent one week with me. He interviewed any oil company official he wanted, from the senior executive of Atlantic Richfield down to BP Oil Company officials, and anyone that he wanted to talk with. They gladly gave him an interview.

I will never forget what he said, the day before he left. He said, Lindsey, I was sitting in the Senate of the State of Colorado when the men came from Washington to brief us as State Senators as to the energy crisis. He said, Lindsey, from what I have seen here this week, from the mockups in the field, from the documentation, and from the people I talked with, I've come to realize that almost everything I was told in that top-level briefing, in the Senate of Colorado, from the men in Washington D.C., that almost everything I was told was the exact opposite from what the truth really is. He said, I was intentionally mis-briefed and I was lied to.

Later, when I wrote the manuscript to my book, *THE ENERGY NON-CRISIS,* I asked him to write the forward to the book. He did. You'll find it recorded there with his name on it.

I'll never forget that day. It was 1976. I walked over to the ARCO base camp, one morning, and as I walked in the front door, there was standing there a gentleman by the name of Jim Waller. He was the equipment man for Atlantic Richfield. And I said, Jim, what's going on today? He said, Chaplain, would you like to really see something exciting? I said, Jim, I'm always in for excitement, what do you mean? He said, come on, hop into the pickup truck, and let's go out to the west dock. He said, I'd like you to see what we think we have struck today. And I said, Jim, what's that?

And as we rode along, he tried to explain: ...that little island out in the ocean, about two and a half miles out from the west dock at Prudhoe Bay, where the floatillar comes in every year. He said, Chaplain, We think we have just struck the largest pool of oil in North America, and maybe the largest pool of oil in the world! Today we're going to release some oil, check the chemical analyses, check the pressure of the field, we already know the size of the field and the depth, and he went on to explain in all of the technical details that an oil man could.

And as we sat there, all of sudden a big black plume of smoke went up into the sky — that was back in the good old days when they let them burn it off at Prudhoe — and after we watched it for a few moments, he said, Chaplain, get in the truck, we have to go back to ARCO base, I want to see what's coming in, from out there at the well site.

I'll never forget that day. And when you hear, as Paul Harvey says, "The Rest Of The Story," you'll know why gasoline could be a dollar fifty cents a gallon at the gas pump in one years time, if only the administration in Washington D.C. would be willing to tell the American people the truth.

We arrived back at base camp. Standing around the desk in Mr. Ken Fromm's office, on the second floor of ARCO base, was the top eight oil company men of the world. I arrived with Jim Long at the door, and Ken Fromm, Senior executive with Atlantic Richfield, said to me, Come on in Chaplain, and they closed the door. And there I stood that day, with men that I never knew I'd rub shoulders with. Here I am a simple aviation missionary out in the bush of Alaska, and all or a sudden I'm standing in the room, watching the "proof" of the largest oil pool in North America, and probably the largest oil pool in the world!

Approximately eight men... if I remember correctly... standing around that table looking at the mockup of the field, looking at the perforations of the pipe, explaining all of the details. I was invited into the room. And Mr. Ken Fromm... after a few moments of excitement, and I've never seen such excited oil men in all my life... they were almost beside themselves. And finally Ken Fromm looked over at me and he said, Chaplain, we have just done it!

I said, Ken, you have just done what? He said, We have just struck the largest pool of oil in North America. It should be headlined on every newspaper in North America tomorrow morning. "American Energy Independent! We don't need any more foreign oil. We can supply from our own soil. We have everything we need." He said, Chaplain, this is the most amazing find we've ever discovered in America!

You can imagine that night. I went back to my dorm room. First thing I wanted to do that morning was to get up and see the headlines on the Anchorage newspaper, it came in on Green Airlines first flight to Prudhoe Bay. I rushed back to ARCO base that morning to have breakfast, and I hardly walked in the door, good, and the security guard caught me and said, Chaplain, don't you say a word to anyone, you go straight upstairs and sit down in Ken Fromm's office. I said, What have *I* done wrong? He said, Don't you even talk to me. You go right up there and sit down. I got orders to catch you as soon as you come in.

I walked into Ken Fromm's office and sat down. A few moments later he walked in, closed the door, sat down across the desk without a smile on his face, and looked up at me and he said, Chaplain, if I were you, I'd be a little careful about what you saw yesterday, and what you say, because, he said, you see, that information about that oil pool out at Gull Island and the Gull Island field, has just been classified. He said, There will be no oil released from it, any time soon.

Oil Beneath Our Feet

3
Alaska's North Slope Oil - Part 3

Rev. Lindsey Williams
January 17, 2007

When my book, *THE ENERGY NON-CRISIS,* came out, there was a chapter in there that alluded to Gull Island. The first edition; this is a *new* updated and *enlarged* edition.

Just after it came out, I had a phone call... maybe two or three months after it came out... from who do you think? Mr. Ken Fromm. The man who was responsible under Atlantic Richfield's leadership to develope the entire east side of the Prudhoe Bay oil field.

I have never heard an oil field man so mad in all my life. He was beside himself. He said, Lindsey, Atlantic Richfield has just fired me. I said, What? You're a career man. You're the head man... You're the senior executive for the development of the oil field. You produced the cracking plant up there at Prudhoe for all the oil up and down the line. You know more about the Prudhoe oil field than anybody. You came up on the RollerCons that came up years ago.

He said, Yes, but Atlantic Richfield just fired me. I said Why, Ken? Because, he said, I was the one who allowed you to see the information that you wrote in you book, *THE ENERGY NON-CRISIS.* Now, he said, Lindsey, You're a missionary, a minister. You're not an oil patch man. And he said, There are a few things in your book that are not letter perfect. He said, I am so angry at Atlantic Richfield, would you allow me rewrite your book for you and make everything letter perfect? I said, Ken, I can't think of anything better. Because, he said, They're going to try to discredit your book on the grounds of a few words that are not right.

For the next thirty days time Ken Fromm and I sat across the table from each other and rewrote this book, *THE ENERGY NON-CRISIS* — and he added a chapter. The only place on the face of this earth that you will find recorded, the largest pool of oil in North America, and probably the largest pool on earth, that our president and vice president... who are oil men... know about and will not tell you the facts.

The only place on the face of the earth you will find it documented, written word for word. They've never been able to question it, nor in any way say that it's incorrect because Ken Fromm... himself... wrote it. The consistency of the oil, the perforations in the pipe, the depth of the field, the pressure of the field, the sulfur content, where it can be refined. It's all right there — the only place you will find on the face of the earth.

Well, this new updated and enlarged edition came out, thanks to Ken Fromm.

About another month later, I had *another* call from him. He said, Well Chaplain, I'm glad I helped you rewrite your book. He said, Atlantic Richfield has just hired me back. They've given me a large increase of pay. They've promised me a bigger retirement. They're sending me to Houston to train all of the executives that come to Prudhoe Bay. From this point on, he said, I won't be able to give you any more information.

He didn't have to. He'd given me enough, because if the oil... watch me now... you need to take this to heart because I'm going to make some very drastic statements in a few moments. You think I've said something, so far. I haven't said anything that you haven't heared me say before, because I've only begun giving this, in the last six months (*Ed. since circa July, 2006*). I decided that I could not keep quiet any longer because your and my freedom is in jeopardy. And unless something is done, America is going to be a "has-been".

Gasoline at the gas-pump, one year from now, here in California, could be less than one dollar and fifty cents a gallon, if the oil that our president and vice president know about, on the north slope of Alaska, were allowed to come to the refineries in America.

Do you know what it costs them to get a barrel... a barrel of oil out of the ground at Prudhoe Bay Alaska? Do you have the slightest idea what it costs Saudi Arabia to get a barrel of oil out of the ground? Well, I hope you have pencil and paper handy, because now I begin with some real nitty-gritty, and you may want to jot down some facts and some figures, because either things are changed with the administration in Washington, D.C., within the next few months — or America will be a "has-been".

Gasoline at the gas-pump in California is going to be four to five dollars a gallon in the very near future.

How do I know?

What I am to say from this point on, you will know that I know what I am talking about.

A little boy went to school, one morning. It was down South. You know how they talk down there, you must recognize that I have a southern accent. The little boy was going to school one day, and the teacher asked the pupils there what they had for breakfast that day. And little Susie spoke up... you know in show and tell... and said, Well, ma'm, I had bacon and eggs for breakfast this morning. It finally came down to little Johnny... a little country boy from way back out on the farm. The teacher said, Johnny, what did *you* have for breakfast this morning? Little Johnny said, Ma'm, I 'et' six biscuits for breakfast today. And the teacher said, Oh, Johnny, that is not correct English, she said, The word is not 'et', it's 'ate'. He said, Well, maybe it **was** eight I 'et'...

Now, I'm going to make you a promise. What I have to say from this point on is **not** going to be a play on words. I'm going to tell... as Paul Harvey says... "The *rest* of the story" that you don't hear in the news, that only a person who sat in the board meetings with these people... sat across the table from them... rubbed shoulders with them for three years... could have known. Things that I have not been willing to tell for the past fifteen years for fear of my own safety. I've decided I cannot keep quiet any longer. So I hope you have those pencils and paper handy.

In the early 60's, crude oil was chosen as the method of controlling the world. It effects every human being. There's only one thing that effects every human being on the face of the earth. The tooth brush that you are going to brush your teeth with tonight before you go to bed is made out of Plastic. What does Plastic come from? Crude oil. The plastic bag in the garbage can that you have in your kitchen, it comes from crude oil. The asphalt highway that you drove on in order to get here to this meeting tonight, it came from crude oil. The drug store... the drugs that you buy, many of them come from crude oil. The shoes that you wear... more than likely they aren't leather... they're probably plastic, it comes from crude oil. The polyester clothes that you are wearing, they are a product of crude oil. The price at the grocery store... and the hardware store... it's going up because of the price of crude oil.

My son and I went to the grocery store the other day. I keep very meticulous records. After all, I have to... being in the business I'm in. If I was not a meticulous person, I wouldn't be able to write the books I have written. And I keep records of what I pay at the grocery store for things.

When I went to the grocery store the other day, every single item without exception had gone up from the previous week. My son and I had to go over to the hardware store and get an item. Daniel was kind of milling around the store, and in a few moments he came over to me, and he said, daddy, you know that step ladder you had your eye on the other day that you wanted to buy, but you just didn't have the funds to buy it? I said, Yes. He said, You should have bought it. I said, Why? He said, It's gone up nineteen dollars.

Now, please write this one down, because it carries great weight with what I'm going to say tonight.

What we pay and the gas pump for a gallon of gasoline is a form of taxation.

Oil Beneath Our Feet

4
Alaska's North Slope Oil - Part 4

Rev. Lindsey Williams
January 17, 2007

Now this is so important, I'm going to say it again. Very few things I repeat twice. What we pay at the gas pump for a gallon of gasoline is a form of taxation that goes to those who control the world, and before I finish my lecture tonight, I'm going to tell you who THEY are. You're going to be surprised. I know what you want me to do. You want me to say certain names, don't you. Well, instead, I'm going to tell it to you as I lived it. Because, you see, what you've read about in other books is not necessarily the truth. You're going to be amazed, at who THEY are.

Gas prices at the gas pump in California WILL BE four dollars to five dollars a gallon at the gas pump in the very near future, and Dr. Stan Montieth, a very reputable radio talk show host, said to me on the phone the other day, Lindsey, you're wrong, it's going to be six and seven dollars a gallon, and it wouldn't surprise me one bit that he's not right, and when it happens, your standard of living in America and mine, is gone, and it's all done by a design plan that I knew about 25 years ago. And I've tried my best to warn the American people for 25 years. This may be your last chance to do something about it.

Those in Washington are scared to death. They're scared to death to tell you the truth. They don't dare tell you the facts. I'm going to in a few moments. And you take it to them. And you try to tell them yourself if you can. Otherwise, we've had it.

Why don't they tell you? Why doesn't president Bush tell you the truth? Why doesn't Mr. Cheney, CEO of Halburton, at one time. He knows it. Why don't they tell you the truth? I'll tell you why. They know what happened to John F. Kennedy when he did. And they shake in their shoes. They know what happened to Larry McDonald on flight 007 when the powers-that-be had him destroyed. They know what happened to George Hansen, the man from Idaho who was in the Congress of the United States of America; they destroyed his family, his home, his position; and after they had totally destroyed him physically and mentally, they patted him on the back and said, Oh, George, go on, we can't find a thing wrong you have done. Every man in Washington knows. Even to some of the Congressmen you respect; and they wouldn't dare tell you the truth. But here it is... It'll be on tape tonight. (*Ed. Oct. 24, 2007*). I have it back on the table, already taped.

There was, back in the 60's... or 70's... a gentleman by the name of Henry Kissinger. He was Secretary of State. He traveled to almost every oil producing country in the world. He went to Saudi Arabia. After all, the Arabs had been nothing but nomads roaming the deserts, riding their camels for many, many years. And he said to them, I'll make you rich. I'd like to cut you a deal. And if you'll go along with my deal, I'll see to it that we buy oil from you, in America.

Now watch carefully, and you'll understand why that oil from the north slope of Alaska cannot be allowed to be brought to the refineries of America. Henry Kissinger said, I'll cut you a deal. Oh, they said, what is it? He said, We'll buy oil from you. We'll make you wealthy. You can have everything you ever wanted. You can be Shakes and Sheiks. Oh, they said, What's the deal? He said, Number One, you must denominate all oil sales in dollars. Oh, they said. Gladly. We have no problem with that. He said, Secondly, you can have a certain percentage of that money to build your own country, your own infrastructure, and the people that are there to supply, for your country, but you must take a certain portion of those American dollars that we buy oil from you with, in American dollars, and buy our national debt.

They didn't have the slightest idea what they were doing when they signed on the dotted line. And today, Saudi Arabia and the other oil producing countries of the world have no choice... they MUST denominate in American dollars and turn around and buy our national debt... It is the only thing that is keeping the American dollar afloat today.

There were two countries that wouldn't sign. Your going to find this very startling... I'm going to give names and dates and places. I never did this prior to six months ago. I've known it for years. You see, it finally gets to a point where you have one of two choices. Either be a slave in your own land, or tell the truth and hope somebody will listen to you. And that's the reason I came here tonight. To try to get a listening ear before it's too late.

There were two countries that wouldn't sign on the dotted line in the days of Secretary of State, Henry Kissinger. Number one, was Iraq. Sadaam... he was too independent. He said, I'm not going to be obligated. The largest known oil field on the face of the earth is Saudi Arabia. Second largest oil field on the face of the earth is Iraq. The third largest oil field on the face of the earth is Iran. I'm going to tell about Iran tonight. You're going to shake in your shoes when you leave from here. I'm not pulling any punches with you this evening. It's either now or never. Either something is done now, or we're slaves in the very near future.

Sadaam said, I'm not going to sign on the dotted line. He

had to be destroyed. Oh, there are a lot of people in the world just as evil as Sadaam. A lot of Russian leaders have killed more people than Sadaam ever did. And yet we joined up with them in the last war. There are a lot of people in the world. Why did Sadaam have to be singled out? Because he wouldn't go along. He wouldn't denominate in American dollars and buy our national debt, and president Bush Sr. had no choice but to destroy him.

Now, there's a name you will want to jot down. The name is Abner Dethrey. I give it to you for one reason and one reason only. He appeared with me on a radio talk show just a few weeks ago. He has never done it before. He worked for the State Department and the CIA, and was one of the individuals that was sent by our State Department to Sadaam Hussein in February and March of 1990 to tell Sadaam Hussein, Our State Department will not intervene if you will invade Kuwait.

It was sent by our own top officials and echelon, to Sadaam that... You do remember that prior to the last war that Iraq and Kuwait were one country, and Sadaam was merely going back in to take back that which had been divided after the last war, and our State Department sent the message by Abner Dethrey, who appeared with me on the radio talk show, as recorded, and he said he took the message to Sadaam from our State Department to tell him, we will not intervene if you invade Kuwait.

It was all a set-up by George Bush Sr., because on August first, 1990, Iraq invaded Kuwait. It was intentional. Our State Department wanted an excuse to topple Sadaam.

5
Alaska's North Slope Oil - Part 5

Rev. Lindsey Williams
January 17, 2007

And they used the invasion which they told Sadaam they would not intervene with, so that George Bush Sr. would have an excuse to invade him. Sadaam was a little too strong for them. George Bush Sr. didn't get elected again. He had to wait eight years. His son got in. He had to finish the job. (*Ed. Long pause. Lindsey deeply moved*). Surprising?

Jot this statement down if you will, please.

The standard currency of the world is oil. Whatever oil is denominated in will determine what the standard currency of the world is. The Federal Reserve Note is nothing but a piece of paper. It is not the standard currency of the world. At one time it was solid. You remember it. Back in 1960 you can take one of these into a bank and buy one of these (*Ed. a silver dollar*). Can you do it today?

A silver dollar now costs $20 to $25 dollars, depending on its quality. That $1 piece of paper will not buy it any more. If Iraq... if we fail... it's not because we don't give them a democracy... you do know that we are not a democracy? "I pledge allegiance to the flag of the United States of America, and to the... REPUBLIC... for which it stands!" Not democracy. A democracy is "We the Sheeple." A republic is "We the People."

They want a democracy given to Iraq because they want control by the oil men of the world, and if they do not succeed, the American dollar is going to be worthless.

It's not the fact that we don't win, it's the fact that if they don't succeed, they have a big, big problem on their hands. Now they're faced with something else. They're faced with Iran... the third largest known oil field on the face of the earth. The Bush-Cheny dynasty is literally milking America for everything it's worth. The powers-that-be have an agenda. They know what they're doing.

I heard them talk about a 30 year plan for the Arabs, when I was the Chaplain of the TransAlaska Pipeline, and I have watched them carry out their plan meticulously without one single flaw. Now, before I give the next startling portion to the lecture, I want to give an example. You will very readily recognize this, and of you who are 50 and above, you'll easily remember back to those days.

In 1984, I had a phone call one day. It was from Mr. Ken Fromm. He was back with Atlantic Richfield down in Houston. You know, even the powers-that-be are sometimes a little proud and haughty, have a good time bragging. And he used to call me up on the phone from time to time, and well, he'd say Lindsey, this, or that, or the other. This time he called me up on the phone he said, Lindsey, are you going to be speaking anywhere around America the next month or two? I said, Yes, Ken. In fact next week I leave to go to Seattle Washington, and about two or three months later to Southern California with speaking engagements.

He said, Well, Lindsey, I'd like you to tell your audience everywhere you go, something that is going to kind of put your speaking on the map. He was bragging... feeling good that day. And I said, Ken, What do you mean? Now, oil at that time was $32 dollars a barrel. We thought it could never go higher or the world would go broke. And he said, Lindsey, I want you to tell your audiences, everywhere you go, that crude oil is going to go down to $10 a barrel. I said, Ken, No. No that can't happen. It would break the Arab world. It would break the oil producing countries of the world. The people would rise up against their leaders and their Shakes and Sheiks. No that can't happen. You can't go down to $10 dollars a barrel.

Ken said very quietly on the phone, Oh, come on Lindsey, come on now, you sat in our board meetings. You know who tells OPEC what we're going to give them for a barrel of oil, you know who's doing this. Now come on, take my word for it. It is going to $10 dollars a barrel.

By the way, do you know what the price of gold was back at that time? $800 dollars an ounce. Remember, it had spiked up to that? The powers-that-be, who had made the Arabs and the other oil producing countries of the world, had said to these wealthy Shakes and Sheiks, and others, they said, "Buy gold." They bought it. They bought it by the train-car-loads. They lined their swimming pools with it. They bought their Roles Royces with it, and their gold. They had everything they wanted, and they paid $700 to $800 dollars an ounce for it, because they'd been told by the people... I'm going to tell you who THEY are before I finish my lecture tonight... to buy gold and they did. You're going to be surprised who THEY are.

They'd been told by those people to buy gold, and they did. But you see, it was all a trap. Just like what's happening right now in our economy. Interest only mortgages on your house is a trap. They know what they're doing. Taking interest down to 1%. It was a trap. They told the Arabs... Buy all this gold... It was a trap.

Ken Fromm said, Lindsey, its going down to $10 a barrel.

I began telling that to my audiences as I arrived in Washington State. Sometimes the people in the audience would literally start giggling. They thought you were crazy. *You* know what you're talking about. When it finally happened and went down to $11 dollars a barrel... it didn't quite go down to $10 dollars a barrel... everybody said you're a prophet. I said, No, I'm not a prophet. I just know the people who are doing it.

You know what the price of gold went to at the same time oil went to $11 dollars a barrel? You remember, what it went to? It went down to $300 dollars an ounce. Who took it there? The same people who are taking it up right now. Why did they take it there? Because they know that the oil producing countries of the world, who had signed on the dotted line, who they'd sold their gold to at $700 and $800 an ounce, would now have to sell it. And they would have to sell it to the same people that they bought it from, in order to maintain their economy, and put food on their tables.

They'd have to sell it back at $300 dollars an ounce. It was all done by a designed manipulative plan and in advance. And I knew it six months before it happened. Because I'd been told by the senior executive of Atlantic Richfield, who kind of chuckled over the phone, and said, Chaplain, come on now, you know who's doing this.

Someone said to me awhile back, Chaplain Williams, don't you think it's time to punch down the cobwebs, and start all over again? I said, No, it's time... to kill the *spider.*

The price of gasoline at the gas pump is a form of taxation imposed by THEM. Who are THEY? You want to *really* know who makes the money that you're paying at the gas pump?

6
Alaska's North Slope Oil - Part 6

Rev. Lindsey Williams
January 17, 2007

Now this will probably be the most startling thing I will say tonight. I'm going to prove to you who THEY are. You see, I knew 25 years ago (*Ed. 2007 - 25 = 1982*). After all, I sat with them and listened to them. I couldn't believe what I was hearing... by the providence of God... no other way.

Who are THEY? Let's start the chain.

Any product... I care not what it may be... there is first of all a manufacturer. Then the manufacturer sells it to a wholesaler. Then the wholesaler sells it to an in-between man, who sells it to the retailer. And the retailer sells it to you. It's a chain. It's true in almost every product, I care not what it is. It is also true in oil, The only thing is, you don't know who the in-between man is, because they don't tell you. But I'm going to, tonight.

First of all there is the oil producing countries of the world. And I'm going to take as an example, the one that you recognize and hear most about, Saudi Arabia. They bring it out of the ground. Do you know what it costs to bring a barrel out of the ground in Saudi Arabia? $5 dollars a barrel. Do you know what it costs to bring a barrel of oil out of the ground at Prudhoe Bay, Alaska? $3 dollars a barrel. I didn't say, transport it. I didn't say refine it, I said "bring it out of the ground." It costs Saudi Arabia $5 dollars... It costs Prudhoe Bay, Alaska, $3 dollars, from our own soil.

Why are you paying $3 dollars a *gallon* at the gas pump, recently? Why are you going to pay $4, $5, and $6 dollars a gallon at the gas pump, in the very near future? Mark my words, you're going to call me on the phone and say, Lindsey Williams, you were a prophet the night you came to this forum. You mark my words, you will. And I'm going to tell you, No... I tried to warn you.

You can't drive these freeways in California at $4 and $5 a gallon and go back and forth to work, and put food on your table. You have to depend on the automobile in California. And you'll be taking food off the table to put in the gas tank, so you can run it out your exhaust pipe. You mark my words, it's already planned. How do I know? Who gets the profit?

First. There's the oil producing country. Then there is someone else that you don't know about. Thirdly, there is the oil company. Oh! All time record profits! We've never seen them making such profits! That's exactly right. They've never made profits like they're making now. But they're not making *anything* like that in-between man makes.

And then there's the little service station attendant. Oh, sure, he's happy when it goes to $3 and $4 dollars a gallon. He's making a few more cents per gallon, and he just thinks that the world has arrived at this house.

Who is the person who is making this big, in-between amount? I know what you want me to do now. You're expecting me to get *ethnic,* don't you? You're expecting me to talk about some *family,* don't you? I'm not going to do it. Because I know better. I know who they are. I lived with them for three years. Who are they? I'm going to call them by name. I'm not beating around the bush. I'm just trying to get you prepared for a startling statement that you probably have never heard before.

Who are they? Who is this in-between person? They sit behind computers in New York and London, every day, and they tell OPEC what they're going to give them for a barrel of oil for that day. They told Ken Fromm that they were going to $10 per barrel. And he called up this little missionary out there in the bush of Alaska, and said, Lindsey, tell the people when you're going around on speaking engagements that we're going to $10 dollars a barrel. How did you know it? Because they knew it. They sit behind the computers in New York and London, every day, and tell every oil producing country in the world what they're going to give them for a barrel of oil, for the day, and they are the *only* ones that know what they're going to give them. And they're making exorbitant profits.

I'd like to give you an example of one of the profits they're making. You heard recently... you probably didn't recognize it... you see the only difference between me and the average person is... I know their buzz words. If you listen to the powers-that-be... you listen to Mr. Greenspan... he tells you the truth... you just don't understand his buzz words.

You listen to the head of Exxon who testified before Congress here just recently. You listen to what he said. You didn't know what he was talking about because you didn't know his buzz words. He everything but told Congress to "get off my back... or else!" I know what the "or else was." Why? Because I lived with them for three years.

Who are they? Remember just recently, you heard on the news... I mean it was all across America... I heard it on the national news. "WORLD BANK, THE IMF, forgive all third world countries their loans." Did they? Did you know what they were talking about? No. You didn't know what they were talking about. I did. Where did they get the money from, to forgive all of those third world countries their loans? Where did they get it from? From the gas pump! $2.50 dollars a gallon... $3 dollars a gallon... you've forgotten the days of 25 cents a gallon, haven't you, back in the 60's? You've got a very short memory. Well, you're going to have a very good memory when it goes to $4 and $5 dollars a gallon, in the very near future, and you can't afford to put it into the gas tank any longer... you're going to remember what I've said here tonight... and wish you'd been taking more action that you've been taking.

Because you see, they could forgive all of those third world countries their loans. They, in turn, can see to it that the national debt of the United States of America is financed through the oil producing countries of the world. They can do every bit of it, because their representatives sit behind the computers in New York and London, every day, and tell the oil producing countries of the world what they're going to give them for a barrel of oil that day. And who are THEY? They're not the oil refineries. You're pointing your finger at the wrong people. And I don't work for them. And I never got one penny of remuneration or any salary when I was on the TransAlaska oil pipeline, I was paid by my Baptist mission board. Alyeska Pipeline Service Company never gave me one penny. I am not obligated in any way. You are pointing the finger at the wrong people. The oil companies are making exorbitant profits. Sure they are. But who's making more than *they* are.

The IMF and the WORLD BANK.

Who forgave the third world countries their loans? The

IMF and the WORLD BANK. How did they do it? You paid it. They diminished our life style in order to give, to those countries. Oh, you think for a moments time, that they're not going to make us on the level of a third world country within the next few years? They sure are. Because you're going to pay for your own demise at the gas pump. There's only one thing that touches the life of every human being on the face of this earth, and that is crude oil. They chose it as a method of controlling the world, in the early 60's, and now the WORLD BANK are the ones that transfer, every day, the transfer of oil from those third world countries, to the oil refineries, and they're the ones making the exorbitant in-between profits. And you will never find it out by reading anybody's book. I would have never known it had I not been there and been told it.

Goldman Sacks predicted that crude oil will reach $105 dollars a barrel. Who makes the profit? The WORLD BANK and the IMF.

Oil Beneath Our Feet

Alaska's North Slope Oil - Part 7

Rev. Lindsey Williams
January 17, 2007

Brazil... Brazil went to the WORLD BANK many years ago and said, We'd like to build Brazilia. We want to make a great nation down here in South America. We need a loan. The IMF said, Sure. We'll be glad to give you a few billion dollars. But we want some collateral. Oh, Brazil said, *Fine,* we own the wealthiest land in the world: the Amazon River Basin. Oh, they said let us have that as collateral, and we'll be more than happy to give you billions of dollars to build your country.

They built Brazilia. They did everything imaginable. Finally, Brazil couldn't quite make it. Like none of these other third world countries can, too well, except Chavez (*Ed. Chavez of Venezuela*) and a few others that wouldn't denominate in dollars. And so Brazil comes back and says, We can hardly even make the interest on the payments. The WORLD BANK said, No problem, we'll be glad to give you *another* line of credit. They didn't give them *any money.* They didn't give them *any silver, any gold,* or *diamonds.* Brazil had all that. What did they give 'em? Computer entries. So the WORLD BANK said, We'll be glad to give you *another* computer entry. We'll give you *another line of credit.* Brazil said, Oh, thank you, thank you. Oh, but they said, Remember. You gave as collateral the Amazon River Basin... Who owns it today? The WORLD BANK. Brazil doesn't own it. They had to give it to them for another line of credit.

Anytime the price of a gallon of gas is over $2 dollars a gallon... we passed that a long time ago... at the gas pump... the people who control the world make over $60 Billion dollars per year. I hope you'll put that figure down.

When crude oil prices increased from $30 to $50 dollars a barrel the world has to shell out an additional $600 Billion dollars a year, to the oil producing countries of the world, who in turn, turn around and buy our national debt.

Now, what is going to effect your life in the immediate future? It's called Iran. It's the third largest oil field in the world.

Iran has said, by a certain date... and by the way that date was given to you tonight by Wendy... I'm not going to repeat it... I will afterwards in questions and answers, if you like... I have a reason for not giving it right now... I'm being careful what I say to you tonight... I know this talk is being recorded.

Iran has said that by a certain date, We are going to flood the world with cheap oil. They have built they're flow-line pipes... they have their ports ready... they already have their oil wells drilled... They have the third largest oil field in the world. They've said they're going to flood the world with cheap oil... and... here's the clincher... we're going to denominate all oil sales in *euros.*

Our president and vice president and congress are shaking in their shoes because they know that if Iran succeeds on the date that they have said, that it will collapse the American dollar. Something must be done with Iran before that date. Watch out.

A lot of people in the world have a nuclear bomb besides Iran. Why don't they go after them? North Korea? Israel?

China? I could go on and on. Why don't they take them on? They have to have an excuse. You see, it was "weapon of mass destruction." Did they exist? Why are they going to take Iran on now? Oh, you'll hear every reason in the world. There's a reason they won't tell you. They know that if Iran succeeds on the date they tell you, it will collapse the American dollar. Because they'll undercut everybody in the world in oil sales.

When President Eisenhouer was President of the United States of America, someone came to him one day and they said, President, Smedly Butler is like you. President Eisenhouer said, No. He had such a great admiration for Major Smedly Butler, he said, *I* would like to be like *him*.

Smedly Butler wrote a book. I'm going to give you a quote out of it.

"War is a racket. It always has been. It is possibly the oldest... easily the most profitable... surely the most vicious... It is the only one in which the profits are reckoned in dollars, and losses in lives. Only a small inside group knows what it's all about. It is conducted for the benefit of the very few, and at the expense of the very many. Out of war, a few people make huge fortunes."

Now, ordinarily authors don't recommend other author's books. I'm going to do so tonight. His name is John Perkins. You must get his book, entitled, *THE CONFESSIONS OF AN ECONOMIC HIT MAN.* It is must reading after what you've heard me say tonight. He says it in a different vein. But he says the same things. John Perkins... I don't know how he's still alive... John Perkins was in insider... he worked for the powers-that-be. In his book he says, "Economic hit men are highly paid professionals who cheat countries around the globe out of trillions of dollars. They funnel money from the WORLD BANK, the United States Agency for International development, and other foreign aid organizations, into the coffers of huge corporations and the pockets of a few wealthy families who control the planet's natural resources. Their tools are fraudulent financial reports, rigged elections, payoffs, extortions, sex, and murder." He should know. He did it. And afterwards had such a guilt conscience that he had to write a book, even if it cost him his life — he is still alive.

Now I'm coming down to the closing... and the punch line.

I'm going to tell you why gasoline cannot be $1.50 a gallon at the gas pump. I'm going to tell you why they cannot allow the Gull Island oil pool to ever come to the American people. But I've got to lead up to it with this. And with that I'm going to close.

Mr. Greenspan, the Federal Reserve Chairman, when he began his tenure in office, the American debt was $1.5 Trillion dollars. Today the debt in the United States of America is... Oh, and we say that he's done such a marvelous job with our economy... Today the debt is $8 Trillion dollars... *plus.* In the month of September... go back... by the way, you can look this up for yourself... the U.S. Treasury Public Debt website... on one day in the month of September... recorded that the national debt went up $60.1 Billion dollars, on that one day. Our present administration, last October... in one month... the Bush administration ran up a national debt of 94.4 Billion dollars, in one month.

OPEC oil producers are at maximum output. Saudi Arabia can't produce any more until they dig some more wells and put in some more flow-line pipe. Every oil refinery in America is operating at 90% capacity. No new refineries have been built in the United States of America for over twenty years, and it's done by a design plan. The U.S. is importing 400,000 gallons of gasoline a day from other countries. The U.S. had 321 refineries in 1981. The U.S. only has 149 refineries today (*Ed. less than half as many as in 1981*). Many plants are operating 24 hours a day with no down time for maintenance, to supply the growing demand. We are operating at 90-plus% output capacity, and the least little bobble, and the gasoline stations would have up signs: "No gas available."

Oil Beneath Our Feet

8

Alaska's North Slope Oil - Part 8

Rev. Lindsey Williams
January 17, 2007

Now here's the rest of the story.

President Bush cannot allow oil from the North Slope of Alaska to come to the United States of America, because if he did the oil producing countries of the world that signed on the dotted line in the days of Henry Kissinger, would not be obligated to take a certain portion of everything that we give them in payment for oil, and turn around and buy our national debt, and the pork in Washington D.C. The $8 Trillion dollar debt would collapse the American economy and the American dollar, therefore our administration today cannot afford to allow you to get the oil from the Gull Island pool, because if they did, and brought it out of the ground at $3 dollars a barrel, and allowed American refineries to refine it, gasoline at the gas pump in American could come down to $1.50 a gallon, or less. But Bush, and the others in Washington, know that it would collapse our economy if they did it. And they cannot tell you the truth.

Somebody must buy our national debt... many others are... not just the oil producing countries... but they alone would cause our dollar to collapse.

Mark my words, you will be paying $4 to $5 dollars a gallon at the gas pump in the very near future. Why? You will be paying for the national debt through the gas pump. You will be paying the third world countries' loans at the gas pump, taking it off the table where your children need food, by a design plan which I knew about 25 years ago, and begged the American people to listen.

Oil Beneath Our Feet

9

Alaska's North Slope Oil - Part 9

Rev. Lindsey Williams
January 17, 2007

Lindsey Williams reveals here why the "oil crisis" is a lie and a power-grabbing scam to get total global control. There is no oil shortage, and gas prices should be below $2 a gallon. (http://tinyurl.com/5yljxa).

The TransAlaska oil Pipeline initially flowed, in 1977, 1.7 million barrels of oil. The field had at that time fifteen hundred pounds of natural artesian pressure. The ecologists said that year that the TransAlaska oil pipeline and Prudhoe Bay oil field will be depleted in twenty years time. Uh, uh. Thirty years later, the field still has fifteen hundred pounds of natural artesian pressure. They're flowing 1.4 million barrels of oil in that pipeline today.

The field has replenished itself! There is no such thing as an Energy Crisis! There is no such thing as a lack of crude oil! And the Russians proved why when they drilled their deep Cola-SG3 wells to forty-two-thousand feet, and finished up the last one, last year, and found in the heart of the earth massive amounts of oil such as man never dreamed of, and the oil fields of the earth, in many areas, are replenishing themselves, just as they're doing now at Prudhoe Bay.

The only lack that we have today is not a lack of oil, it's a lack of honesty in Washington D.C.

There is enough natural gas on the north slope of Alaska to supply the entire United States of America for over 200 hundred years if every other natural gas well in the nation were cut-off tomorrow morning. One billion cubic feet of natural gas are being pumped back into the ground at Prudhoe Bay Alaska every day by using (48) 747 type jet aircraft engines because the government of this United States will not allow another pipeline to be built down the same corridor as the TransAlaska oil pipeline, Though not disturbing the ecology in any manner, and supplying for America cheap natural gas for the generation of electricity and the heating of your homes.

It's an *atrocity* that should cause such an uprising among the American people that there would be an impeachment from our president on down!

You see, if we were allowed to have the oil from the North Slope of Alaska to come to American refineries, the price of gasoline at the gas-pump could plummet as much as $1.50 a gallon. But our president cannot allow it. And they will *never* open up ANWAR (*Ed. the Arctic National Wildlife Refuge in Northeastern Alaska*).

Why won't they? Because if they allowed the oil from our own soil to come to American refineries the other pro-ducing countries of the world that have not jumped-ship, yet, would not be obligated to buy our national securities and T-bills — and our dollar would collapse in a month's time. And our president knows it.

But yet, on the other hand, if other nations continue to jump-ship and don't use the American dollar, and the New York bankers no longer have the control of the oil of the world through the control of the America dollar, the dollar will collapse anyway. It's just a matter of time. It's going to happen, one way of the other.

Had you rather have back the great American Dream and some honesty in Washington D.C., and let the dollar collapse if necessary, and then start all over again?

I think it's time to kill the spider, don't you?

Oil Beneath Our Feet

Drilling In ANWR

Oil Beneath Our Feet

10
ANWR
Arctic National Wildlife Refuge

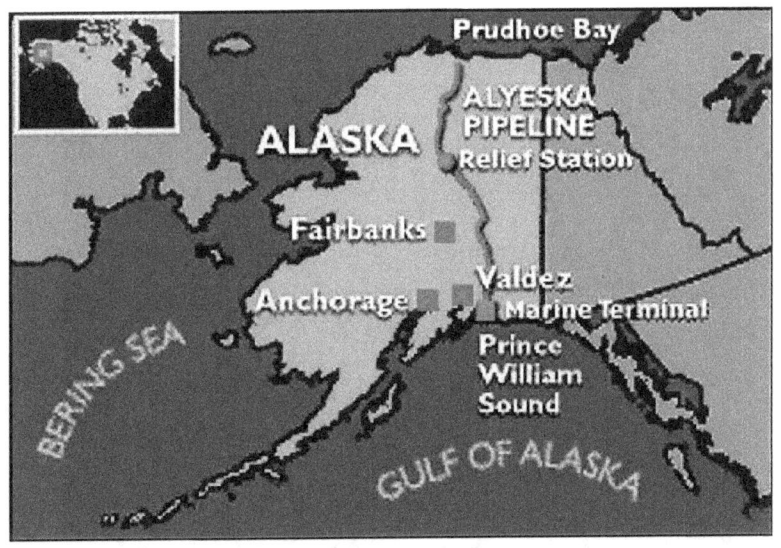

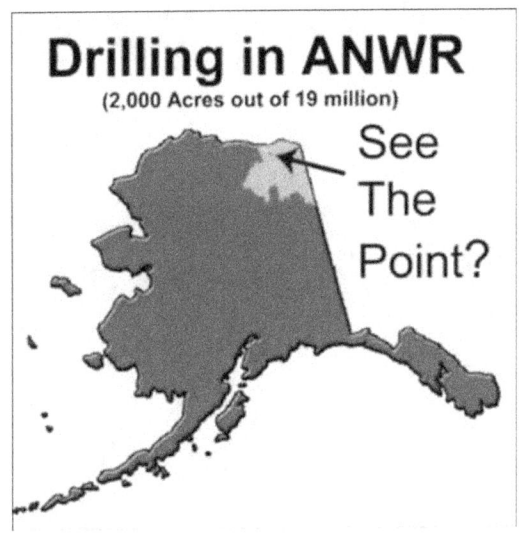

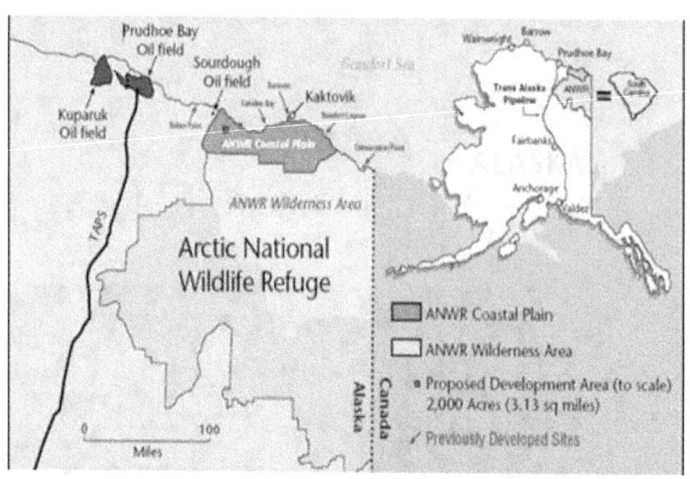

Oil Beneath Our Feet

Isn't ANWR beautiful? Why should we drill here in this beauiful place? Well that's not exactly where they intend to drill. The Map on the previous page shows that the proposed drilling area is in **the ANWR Coastal Plain.** Did those photographs look like a Coastal Plain to you? What's going on here? The answer is simple: **That is not where they are wanting to drill.**

This is what the PROPOSED exploration area looks like in the winter.

America's Energy Non-Crisis!

As you can see, the area where they are wanting to drill **is a barren wasteland;** and they say that they are concerned about the effect on the local wildlife.

Does this bear act like he's afraid?

Oil Beneath Our Feet

Here is another shot of what the PROPOSED exploration area looks like in the winter.

Here is a photo of **the socalled "Depleted Wildlife" situation** created by drilling around Prudhoe Bay... Don't you suppose that the Caribou are afraid and really hate that drilling?

The Prudhoe bay area accounts for 17% of U.S. domestic oil production

NOW, WHY DO YOU THINK THAT THE
DEMOCRATS ARE
LYING ABOUT ANWR?

REMEMBER WHEN AL GORE SAID
THE GOVERNMENT SHOULD WORK TO
ARTIFICIALLY
RAISE GAS PRICES TO $5.00 A GALLON?

WELL... AL GORE AND HIS FELLOW
DEMOCRATS HAVE ALMOST
REACHED THEIR GOAL!

NOW THAT YOU KNOW THAT THE
DEMOCRATS HAVE BEEN LYING,
WHAT ARE YOU GOING TO DO ABOUT IT?

YOU CAN START BY SHARING THIS
WITH EVERYONE YOU KNOW...
SO THAT THEY WILL KNOW THE TRUTH.

11
Oil Fictions Exposed

THE FICTION: That Domestic Drilling Won't Have Impact for Ten Years or More.

According to Senator Barack Obama and Congressional liberals allowing more domestic drilling won't have any impact on energy prices for ten years or more. No. That is not correct.

Recent Moves toward Greater Domestic Drilling Have Dramatically Reduced Energy Prices in Just one Month.

In the month since President Bush rescinded the executive order prohibiting drilling on the Outer Continental Shelf (OCS) and the Arctic National Wildlife Refuge (ANWR), the price of oil has already plummeted. From its record high of over $145 per barrel in July when Bush signed the order, the price has tumbled some 21% to $115 in one short month.

This is because the market price for oil partially reflects future supply expectations. Accordingly, any movement toward reliable, secure, domestic sources of oil and gas sends the signal of increased future supply. This helps offset current uncertainties surrounding such volatile oil-and gas-producing areas as the Persian Gulf, Venezuela, Russia and Nigeria, thereby assuring energy markets of a more dependable flow of future energy.

In other words, potential disruptions in the aforementioned regions undermine energy source reliability and add to the current market price. In contrast, taking steps to assure a greater supply of safe, reliable, domestic sources in such places as ANWR and the OCS bolsters energy source reliability and helps reduce the market price.

Obviously, President Bush's wise decision isn't the sole reason for oil's recent decline. A stronger dollar, the slowing world economy and reduced demand have also played a role. But the reality is that the world economy was already slowing before July, and demand was already being reduced while the price of oil continued its march toward record highs.

Furthermore, keep in mind that the price of oil has declined since President Bush's order despite such new geopolitical turmoil as Russia's invasion of Georgia, which sits in an energy-rich area and is a critical conduit of oil.

You've got to give Obama and Congressional liberals like Nancy Pelosi credit for trying, though. After all, in the ongoing debate about whether to allow more domestic drilling to reduce energy prices and America's unhealthy dependence upon foreign oil, they're running out of rationalizations.

Originally, they found it safe to oppose domestic drilling in places like ANWR on the basis that it would spoil beautiful, pristine environments. That excuse was of limited value, when voters realized that ANWR is a desolate, distant moonscape the size of South Carolina, where only an area the size of Dulles International Airport would be drilled. Voters also realized that the threat of horrendous offshore oil rig spills on the OCS is extremely remote, since even Hurricane Katrina failed to cause such catastrophes in the Gulf of Mexico.

Drilling opponents later contended that oil companies

aren't drilling in oil-abundant areas on which they already hold leases. But voters quickly wised up to the reality that the leased areas on which drilling hasn't occurred simply don't yield enough oil or gas to justify enormous expenses to extract them.

Faced with this inconvenient truth, so to speak, Senator Obama retreated to arguing that more domestic drilling is a mere "scheme" that won't have any impact for a decade or more. Unfortunately for him, events over the past 30 days have obliterated that misrepresentation as well.

Now, pundits are rationalizing that the recent oil price decline is the result of Americans driving fewer miles or buying fewer sport utility vehicles. And indeed, Americans drive 3.7% fewer miles than they did one year ago, and we purchased 7% fewer SUVs than one year ago. But those declines have occurred over an entire year, and hardly account for a 21% drop in just one month since July.

Indeed, American consumers began reducing their miles driven back in November 2007, yet oil and gasoline prices continued to ascend until just last month. Moreover, the price decline occurred during the height of summer vacation driving season, not an off-peak driving month. Therefore, one can't attribute oil's rapid decline to Americans abandoning the highways.

The simple fact is that greater domestic energy production will substantially assist America's effort to reduce energy prices that are burdening American families, and decrease our dependence upon foreign energy sources. Voters have come to this realization, and now support domestic exploration by widening majorities.

Rather than face this reality and do the right thing, however, Nancy Pelosi and Harry Reid decided to call a recess and abandon Washington in order to obstruct progress on this matter. But neither their parliamentary schemes nor Senator Obama's mischaracterizations (lies) will succeed in obscuring the reality that we must drill here, drill now.

They are out of excuses. Now, they must finally act or face the consequences in November.

12
Is Too Much Oil
An Economic Threat?

From the July 26, 2008 International Forecaster:
www.theinternationalforecaster.com

Lindsey Williams, who has been an ordained Baptist minister for 28 years, went to Alaska in 1971 as a missionary. The Transalaska Oil Pipeline began its construction phase in 1974, and because of his concern for the spiritual welfare of the "pipeliners," Mr. Williams volunteered to serve as Chaplain on the pipeline, with the subsequent full support of the Alyeska Pipeline Company.

Because of the executive status accorded to him as Chaplain, he was given access to the information that is documented in his book, "The Energy Non-Crisis"...

http://tinyurl.com/24ug7h

...which shows that peak oil is a scam because our domestic reserves in the North Slope of Alaska, alone, are at least as large as those in Saudi Arabia and are potentially large enough to power the US with domestic oil for two hundred years. Recently this year, due to the sensitive nature of his book, *Mr. Williams' life was threatened and he was forced to shut down his web-site and stop selling his books and CDs.* At the urging of Dr. Stanley Monteith of Radio Liberty...

http://www.radioliberty.com

...*Williams* called back the same oil executive who had

warned him about the danger he would be in if he continued to disseminate certain information, to ask if in fact there was any information that he could in fact convey to the public without upsetting the powers-that-be. The oil executive, who Mr. Williams had known for years, gave Mr. Williams some startling revelations which he could safely reveal to the general public. As you know, the Illuminati are arrogant enough to reveal *some* of their plans because they believe there is nothing we can do about it.

The Energy Non-Crisis Video - by Lindsey Williams
http://tinyurl.com/33l95c

Basically, Mr. Williams was told that over the next twelve months, from mid-2008 to mid-2009 . . .

(1) that news of super giant oil fields, ready to produce, would be announced for two locations, in the Northern Slopes of Russia and in Indonesia, which oil fields would together contain more oil reserves than the entire Middle East;

(2) that this news would drive oil prices down to $50 per barrel;

(3) that OPEC countries, especially in the Middle East, would be bankrupted by this price decrease;

(4) that this would cause the financing of our foreign trade and current account deficits (through purchases of treasury paper by foreign nations with their surplus oil profits) to collapse, leading to the collapse of the dollar;

(5) that the collapse of the dollar would cause unprecedented financial strife and turmoil in the US, and that it would take many years for the US to recover from this financial debacle;

(6) that they (big oil) support John McCain for President; and

(7) that US domestic oil reserves would never be tapped, and that any legislation which might allow domestic reserves to be tapped, would not be allowed to pass, leaving the US dependent on foreign oil forever.

News of the Russian oil field has been announced just as predicted, but whether the rest happens as stated above remains to be seen. Nevertheless, many of these revelations seem quite feasible, so we thought we would comment on how these revelations might play out, under the current financial scenario.

Certainly, if the world's oil reserves ready to produce are increased by an amount equal to the total oil reserves of the Middle East, oil could easily be brought down to $50 per barrel. It would almost be like starting all over again from an oil reserve perspective. This would destroy the economies of countries that are currently giving us trouble, such as Iran and Venezuela, allowing us to defeat them without ever firing another shot. Russia would get less per barrel, but would be selling an awful lot of oil out of their vastly increased reserves, so they would be weakened, but not bankrupted.

Nations in the Middle East, whose reserves are rapidly dwindling, would all be destroyed from an economic perspective at first, but the ensuing civil unrest would also eventually topple all Middle East OPEC regimes, allowing the US to move in and take over control of their governments and their remaining oil reserves.

Countries such as China, Japan and India, who import large portions of their oil, would get a huge shot in the arm from reduced oil prices, and this would also be a great help to the free-trade, globalization agenda, which is being strained by high oil prices because transportation costs are offsetting the advantages of cheap labor.

What we envision happening under the scenario revealed to Mr. Williams would certainly start with the stated reduction in oil prices well ahead of elections.

This would produce great joy and relief for the Sheeple and ignite a huge, worldwide stock market rally just prior to elections, making George Bush and congressional incumbents look a lot better and lending support to John McCain, the stated preferred presidential candidate of big oil.

Much lower oil prices would support the dollar and suppress precious metals by reducing inflation by the amount attributable to recent oil price increases, but only at first. The huge rally would give the elitists the chance they were looking for to bail out of paper assets such as stocks, bonds (which would include treasuries) and derivatives at the top of the markets using the dark pools of liquidity known as "Project Turquoise" and "Baikal."

The proceeds from the sale of paper assets would then be plowed into real, tangible assets such as commodities, precious metals, real estate, infra-structure, machines and equipment and corporations whose values are heavily weighted in tangible assets, such as resource stocks.

The prices of such real, tangible assets would be bought on the cheap due to their ongoing suppression, or at least that would be the Illuminati's hope, but we see most of these items skyrocketing long before the elitists get their fill of these goodies.

Many nations with large foreign reserves, like China,

Japan and Germany, and especially nations "friendly" to the US, such as Saudi Arabia, who would be hurt by lower oil prices, would be given free reign to invest in tangible, real assets of the US, and this ties in with the cessation of the Federal Trade Commission's publication of statistics regarding foreign investment in the US, as a cover-up for this huge flood of foreign money.

These foreign investment reports were allegedly discontinued because such reports cost too much to produce, but essentially this is the same bologna we got from the Fed when they discontinued the publication of M3, to cover up their profligate issuance of money and credit.

All this money pouring into tangible, real assets from the sale of paper assets through dark pools of liquidity *outside the view of the public and outside the view of non-insider institutional investors* would then ignite a fresh round of wildly spiraling inflation.

Such hyperinflation, compounded by direct monetization of treasuries by the Fed to bail out big commercial banks and other financial institutions, including Fannie and Freddie, and to finance burgeoning foreign trade and current account deficits caused by the cessation of foreign investment in treasury paper, would take us to a historical reenactment of Germany's former Weimar Republic and today's Zimbabwe. The dollar would collapse, along with our economy, and stock, bond and derivative markets would be devastated. The public, as usual, would be left holding the bag, precisely as happened in the days leading up to the Stock Market Crash of 1929 and the ensuing Great Depression.

As an aside, all *insiders* were warned early in 1929

when to get out of the market (i.e. when the Fed was going to turn off the money and credit spigot) while all *non-insiders* were left like lambs for the ensuing slaughter. Rest assured that the elitists are planning a repeat of that rip-off, but on a much *grander* scale.

During the Great Depression, FDR outlawed ownership of gold in the US, but elitist insiders were warned of this in advance and moved their gold holdings overseas. FDR then raised the redemption rate for an ounce of gold from $20 to $35, giving the elitist insiders an instant 75% profit, showing that crime *does* pay, and it pays well, when you are a part of the group of reprobates and sociopaths who comprise or support the Illuminati.

This type of treatment of public gold holdings will most likely not happen under the current scenario, because US citizens hold very little gold, the gold standard has been eliminated, and most of elitist gold holdings are now held overseas, in any case, especially in Switzerland. Also, gold bullion holdings of the US treasury have all been stolen, leased, swapped out or otherwise compromised. That is why our *so-called* gold "reserves" have not been properly audited since 1954, and why they are referred to as "deep storage gold" in the US Mint's and Treasury Department's statements of account.

Elitists may use their thousands of tons of failsafe gold, which, incidentally, they have acquired over the ensuing decades either by stealing them from national treasuries or by buying them at fire-sale prices, such as the bargains made available through Gordon Brown's sale of the UK's national gold at the bottom of the market, to back a new regional currency for North America such as the proposed

Amero, once the dollar has been destroyed.

Getting back once again to Mr. Williams' scenario:

In order to protect scum-bag incumbents *who always do whatever the Illuminati tell them to do because they are bought-and-paid-for, or compromised,* the elitists would attempt to support the dollar and prevent it from collapsing prior to elections. They would do this by temporarily stemming the flood of foreign investment in tangible, real assets located within the US and by getting certain nations like China and Japan to keep buying up treasuries by giving them sweetheart deals on such future investments in tangible, real assets located in the US, especially on real estate, infrastructure and investment in surviving elitist financial institutions and transnational conglomerates.

Many Arab nations would break their dollar pegs, but would delay doing so until after elections based on promises of security for what will be their outgoing regimes once their economies collapse from cheap oil prices. This could be why Paulson and Bernanke are flying around the globe meeting with various heads of state, namely, to arrange all of the above.

Once the new round of hyperinflation gets started, the dollar would be destroyed and replaced with a new currency such as the amero which would be the de facto start up of the North American Union, which the elitists continue to vehemently deny is a work-in-progress for the US, Canadian and Mexican governments.

During the ensuing financial conflagration, the elitists would attempt to nationalize many industries, and take control over the entire financial sector through the Fed or its successor which may be planned by the Illuminati.

Civil unrest may ensue in the US, and this would be used to increase police state powers, perhaps through the implementation of martial law, which has all been set up in the Patriot Acts and the Military Commissions Act. Off to the concentration camps will go all the truth-seeking and truth-disseminating troublemakers while the rest of the Sheeple are led blindly around with a ring in their nose to wherever the elitists decide to take them.

The troublemakers have already been identified by the CIA, NSA, Pentagon and FBI using Project Echelon and scads of illegal wire-taps and other nefarious spying techniques which the Bush Administration has rampantly implemented in pursuance of a surveillance society and Nazi-like police state.

The end result that is planned is a corporatist, fascist state that would make Mussolini and Hitler green with envy. Next comes the elimination of the "useless eaters" and the creation of Plato's vision, which is George Orwell's "1984" *on steroids,* the ultimate worldwide feudal system.

The above scenario is not without its problems, however. Lower oil prices reduce elitist profits, and could put a big hit on struggling elitist financial institutions that are exploiting the Enron loophole and cheap credit from the Fed to save their balance sheets. However, once the Illuminati control the world's oil, they can price oil as high as they like using whatever excuse suits them at the time, just as they have done for decades.

But control over oil in Russia and Indonesia may be problematic, since these regimes are not typically friendly to US interests. Further, confrontations may occur with China, India and other big oil importers who may feel that their continuous supply of oil would be under constant threat if the Illuminists controlled most of the world's reserves, and some of those big oil consumers may try to cut deals with the bankrupted nations in OPEC as a failsafe against Illuminist control, assuming that such bankrupted nations are able to shirk off Illuminist attempts to take them over. This may entail much war and conflict, which the financially strapped US is unable to handle with its stretched-to-the-limit military. Also, civil unrest and protests may get out of control in the US and abroad, and the Illuminati may get a much bigger backlash than they are planning.

People are going to get wise to what has been done to them, and a good number of them are going to do something about it. Many Illuminists may start to disappear without a trace if people start to get their dander up, and the civil unrest may spiral beyond elitist control.

Further, the Illuminati are very vulnerable due to the credit-crunch, asset-backed derivative and real estate debacles plus the inevitable addition of a quadrillion dollar, smoldering caldera of interest rate and credit default swaps.

Also, what would happen if certain nations did not cooperate, and started to buy precious metals and commodities with their sovereign wealth funds or broke their dollar pegs too soon. It's not as easy as it might first appear, and we can always count on the forces of "Chaos" to show the same acumen as those in the old "Get Smart" series, so the Illuminati really have their work cut out for them. We believe they will ultimately fail, and that world government will once again become a far-in-the-future objective for the would-be lords of the universe.

If you don't own gold, silver and their related shares under the Williams scenario, you will quite simply be vaporized.

The rollover process for COMEX gold futures got underway this week, which is why gold is showing some weakness, in addition to lower manipulated oil prices and dead-cat PPT dollar rallies that will soon peter out. This process will be complete by the end of July, and then its "Katie-bar-the-door" against the explosion in precious metals prices.

Earnings will continue to disappoint, the credit-crunch will worsen, bank failures will continue to occur, the dollar and assets denominated in dollars will continue to be shunned, ardent de-leveraging will continue unabated, keeping pressure on the stock markets, the real estate market will continue to worsen and derivatives will soon implode as inflation spirals out of control, consumer spending drops into nothingness and real interest rates continue to rise, giving rise to a potential bear market in bonds that could bring the whole Illuminist financial house of cards tumbling down, as their main source of power explodes and goes down in flames like the Hindenberg.

The Fed continues to be irrelevant because their power over real interest rates is greatly diminished. The Fed's governors are boxed in, and cannot get out, as their European counterparts take rates in the opposite direction. The Fed governors would really like to go if it would not stoke inflation in the process. The fraudsters will continue to fail, and the Sheeple will continue to bail, unless we rise up and do something about it.

Throwing out all incumbents would be a good start.

13
Abiotic vs. Biotic

abiotic: adj. originating from sources other than biological organisms.

biotic: adj, origination from plant or animal life, or other biological organisms.

A number of geologists and planetary scientists no longer believe that oil is a product from the conversions of biotic (once living) sources, but is an ongoing abiotic process occurring continuously deep within the earth — in a region described by the late astrophysicist, Thomas Gold, as *"The Deep Hot Biosphere"* — in his book by the same name.

Dr. Gold was the Austrian Astrophysicist who perfected radar during the Second World War. He was Head of Cornell University's Astronomy Department in 1959, and he won the Gold Medal of the Royal Astronomical Society in 1985.

The conversion of carbon and hydrogen into molecules of various hydrocarbons is now thought to be possible in abiotic oil formation at extreme depths. Here, according to abiotic theorists, carbon and hydrogen combine to form methane which in turn form the multitudes of hydrocarbon chains we know as petroleum — or crude oil.

Being lighter than the surrounding rock, the hydrocarbons are buoyed upwards toward the surface, but are usually stopped by an impenetrable layer we call bedrock. There they may accumulate indefinitely until a fissure occurs, allowing them to further rise toward the surface where they then often pool in sedimentary rock.

One of the causes of fissures is the impact of asteroids or comets, such as that which caused the Chicxulab Crater on the Yucatan peninsula in Mexico and is often associated with the extinction of the dinosaurs. This collision fractured the bedrock in the Gulf of Mexico in an area where major oil fields are found, including what was thought to be the second largest oil field on Earth, the Cantarell Field, discovered in 1976 by a fisherman of that name who thought he was fishing over a sunken boat leaking fuel oil.

Similarly, the bedrock beneath Saudi Arabia is seriously fractured, and abiotic theorists claim that major oil fields in that country are directly over the fissure lines.

The predominant theory of "rock-oil formation" (petroleum), called "fossil fuel," was challenged in the late 19th century. Then the 1950s brought forth serious studies from Russian and Ukrainian scientists that resulted in the Russian and Ukrainian Theory: that "the preponderance of geological evidence compels the conclusion that crude oil and natural petroleum gas have no intrinsic connection with biological (biotic) matter originating at or near the surface of the earth. That they are primordial material which has risen to the surface from great depths."

Since then, the Soviets, and now the Russians, have put their money where their theory was and now is, and reportedly have been highly successful in developing oil fields where other petroleum geologist feared to tread. Dr. Gold convinced the Swedish State Power Board to spend $25 million to prove or disprove the abiotic theory, by drilling in areas of volcanic and other non-sedimentary bedrock where no plant or animal life ever existed. While not enough crude oil was found to be commercially viable, petroleum was indeed located where most geologists thought it not to be possible.

The *London Telegraph* quipped in its obituary for Dr. Gold that this was "an achievement in the same league as Moses' getting water from a stone."

At present, however, successful drilling in areas heretofore considered barren of hydrocarbons will not be information to be announced to the world. Such knowledge would more than likely destroy the generally held belief that we are running out or oil, the primary reason why OPEC members can charge more that $100 dollars for a barrel of oil that can cost $5 dollars to bring it out of the ground.

Anyone with oil and gas leases, options, or mineral rights will have to make serious adjustments if and when the current artificial price structure of cuide oil collapses, as eventually it will.

"The time for thinkers has come." (*S&H vii:13*) Consider the facts. Americans are not being told the truth.

Note what Rev. Lindsey Williams said at the beginning of his report . . .

Russia has just drilled some, what they call, super-deep wells to the depths of some 42,000 feet; super-deep wells which they call Cola-SG3. They have found massive amounts of oil. The world is nowhere near running out of crude oil. — (*page 9*).

And what Williams said at the end of his report . . .

The TransAlaska oil Pipeline initially flowed, in 1977, 1.7 million barrels of oil. The field had at that time fifteen hundred pounds of natural artesian pressure. The ecologists said that year that the TransAlaska oil pipeline and Prudhoe Bay oil field will be depleted in twenty years time. Uh, uh. Thirty years later, the field still has fifteen hundred pounds of natural artesian pressure. They're flowing 1.4 million barrels of oil in that pipeline today. — (*page 49*).

And Williams continues . . .

>   ***The field has replenished itself.*** *There is no such thing as an Energy Crisis! There is no such thing as a lack of crude oil!*
>
>   And the Russians proved why, when they drilled their deep Cola-SG3 wells to forty-two-thousand feet, and finished up the last one last year, and found in the heart of the earth massive amounts of oil such as man never dreamed of, and ***the fields of the earth,*** in many areas, ***are replenishing themselves,*** just as they're doing at Prudhoe Bay.
>
>   The only lack that we have today is not a lack of oil, it's ***a lack of honesty in Washington D.C.***

The oil crisis is a lie, a power grabbing scam to get total Global control. There is no oil shortage. Gas prices at the pump should be below $1.50 a gallon, right now!

Fusion vs. Fission

The following two chapters <u>transcribe</u> the non-technical parts of a lecture on *"Alternative Fusion Energy"* given as a Google Tech Talk on Nov. 9, 2006 by Princeton PHD Robert Bussard, Co-Founder/Director of ENERGY/MATTER CONVERSION CORP. (EMC^2).

http://tinyurl.com/y8eq8h8

14
Fusion vs. Fission - Part 1

Robert Bussard, PHD
November 9, 2006

I'm really pleased to see all of you interested in something that if it works will help a lot of us on this planet. I started out in the Engineering and R&D business 57 years ago in the space flight era, and rockets and space were the things that moved me, and that's what caused me to get into frontier technical development, which led me down this long trail to this fusion program.

I'm going to talk about, *"What is Nuclear Fusion?"* How it's different from fission and fission's problems, and what we did in our small company . . . we actually named it, ENERGY/MATTER CONVERSION CORPORATION, because we liked the fact that Einstein had invented it and it's formula EMC^2, and we have a registered trademark . . .

what we learned from our work and our general conclusions . . . and then at the last, Why are we doing this? What is it good for? It's not just scientific entertainment. We're not doing it to make money. We're doing it for a particular goal (which *will* make a lot money) and how to get there, and what the next steps will have to be, in how to get to the end of the road.

I'm making an assumption, and I may be wrong, that a lot of you are not familiar with the details of fission and fusion energy, because you're in the "it" business, but that may be wrong, and I apologize to those of you who find that this is boring.

Fusion is the energy that powers everything in the universe. It's the action that make solar energy. Every photon that falls on the earth comes down from the sun; from a **fusion** reactor.

Fission takes place when heavy atoms are split into two radio-active atoms.

Fusion takes place when two light atoms merge into something that splits.

Fission creates the radio-active isotopes that gave us Three-Mile Island and Chernoble and containment isotopes we can't control.

Fusion energy is released when light nuclear are fused. The intermediate product fissions into light atoms that are not radio-active. The ultimate fuels use *hydrogen-nuclear together,* and that's what runs the sun. Other common light elements can do that too. (*ed. be made to fuse and release energy*). These include lithium, boron, and helium isotopes. Some **fusion** reactions are radiation-free whereas others are not.

I want to show you the energy levels.

We all know by chemistry that fire . . . hydrogen and oxygen burning . . . makes H^2O and gives you about 10 electron units of energy. If you take deterium and tridium . . . the two heaviest isotopes of hydrogen . . . and use them to make a helium foreign neutron, you get 17,600,000 electron units of energy (*ed. compared to 10 electron units; a multiple ratio of 1,760,000: 1 !*).

Fission's chain-reaction gives you Hiroshima, Nagasaki, and all the "excitement" of the world.

Fusion is different. **Fusion** makes one of the most stable carbons in the universe. When it's *excited* by the binding energy of the **fusion** process, it decays to helium'4, and a fraction of a second later, into two *more* helium'4s . . . so this process is *unique.*

Fusion is the only *nuclear energy releasing process* in the world that releases **fusion** energy as *three helium atoms,* and no *neutrons, no radiation . . . it's radiation free!* Which means that if you build a machine that runs on that **(fusion)**, you can turn it off, and go sit on it, and there'll be no *Three-Mile Islands,* and no *Chernobles.*

Four machines would make Utilities feel happy, we think the best one is the DT **Fusion** System that makes a lot of process steam. You could put a number of them, *lined up in a row,* in the central part of a power plant, in a Reactor Building, with the rest of the plant as a normal plant, with steam-powered-electrical-generators, cooling towers, etc. This is the way you can 'retro-fit' existing fossil-fuel-fired-plants.

Build a little Reactor Building, and tie into existing steam lines, and leave the fuel tanks there and turn the oil tanks off, and run the thing on the steam that comes from the DT **Fusion** System.

It's no different than a PWR System, except when you turn it off, there isn't any *isotope product* to decay and kill you.

What we found for the Navy was we can make a small, efficient, power reactor 1/3rd the size of current magnetic confinement reactors. In the long run the Navy is interested in PB11, a way to make an electric [run] ship that has no radiation like existing nuclear submarines have, with relatively simple engineering, commercial viability of about 6-10 years from the time they prove the first main demo-plant, at the cost today of from $80-120 million, to fit in the power bay of an "Arleigh Burke Destroyer." It would run for as many years as the electrical systems would hold up.

We did most of our work for the Navy. They had to fund this at the lowest level, below the radar screen of politics, and that's exactly what happened. The DOE (*Department of Energy*) would see it and say, "No, *WE* have the charter to do **fusion**." They would co-opt it, and shut the Navy's effort down. There you have it. **It's nature. It's life.** Funding has *always* been way too small.

No one in the government is interested in doing this. The government will always turn to *government labs* and the *labs* will say, No!

I've given up on the government; the Navy's budget was cut off.

There's no-one at the DOE who will ever support it . . . not until it's running in China . . . because of . . . It's a threat.

It's a threat to the $2 million a day ISPOL [*Ice Station Polarstern Atmosphere Ice Ocean Interactions*] and every one is pounding down the road for it to be built in France. This is the next big thing. *They can do research on it for the next 30 years and retire on it.*

There's no way, with the current budget situation in Iraq, and the current administration, to get anybody interested in anything except *700 mile fences and the Iraq war,* and one thing and another. That's what it is. *There's no way the DOE will do it.*

I don't see government doing it anywhere in any of the Western nations. That's why I limit the overseas nations to nations that are **not** partners in the TOCAMAK program. There are **enough** of them and at an average of $40 million a year [each] it can be done by a *lot of different countries . . . and probably will be . . .* if we don't do it.

We have the patents on it; [and] there are a lot of people in the world that don't have the kind of **mental constraints** that we have in this country, and for all I know, **that's the way it will happen.**

These things will make space engines 1,000 times better than anything else! Single-stage to Mars in 4 weeks! Seventy-six days to Titan (*one of the moons of Saturn*).

It's a very remarkable engine!

The **fusion community** is so old and so entrenched. You always run against them; they would say, *"How come if it's so good, the [U.S.] government isn't doing it ?"*

Oil Beneath Our Feet

15
Fusion vs. Fission - Part 2

Robert Bussard, PHD
November 9, 2006

Now I want to talk about, *"Why are we doing all this? Who Cares?"* Are we doing this for fun . . . the Navy . . . or the DOD (*Dept. of Defense*)?

We're a one contract company . . . a sole source contractor from the beginning. We've *never* had but one contract, which, of course, is why we died when the money failed. But if we can make it work. We can overcome global environmental problem needs . . .

- we can stop the greenhouse effect.
- we can end the generation of atmospheric smog.
- we can eliminate the sources of acid rain.
- we can decrease the sources of thermal pollution.
- we can end the production of nuclear waste.
- we can burn-up nuclear waste inventories.
- we can end water shortages for every nation.

You can build a DT System that will make so many neutrons that you can burn up the nuclear waste of 20 power plants in steady state time and make power at the same time, and sell it, and change the storage time from 4,000-9,000 years down to 40-90 years, which is more tractable.

It's an *inexhaustible source!* Hydrogen is everywhere. Neutrium is everywhere. Neutrium is 1-part in 6,000-parts in every glass of water you drink.

Electric fusion plants provide cheap, fuel-free, electric power in clean, low-cost systems.

You can make cheap ethanol and replace gasoline. A 50,000-ton barge off the coast of Brazil can produce 6,000-tons of ethanol, a day, with a thirty-eight square-mile cane field, growing two crops a year. You can ferment the pith as well as the juice, and make wood products out of the of the husk, all at $0.24 to $0.30 cents a gallon. ***But the big oil companies might not like it unless you gave them a license to do it.*** All the Third World countries in the tropics where you can get two crops a year can become oil producers. ***Very interesting!***

We were embargoed [censored] from writing papers about what you could do with this if you had it . . . make rocket propulsion and space flight practical. It will bring global economic stability . . . and that's really the main driver.

Global Economy 101

Fusion would . . .

• make Cheap, Clean, Thermal Electrical Power readily available.

• fix energy prices to stabilize the economy,

• stop OPEC ups and downs.

• . . . low value cane in Third World countries becomes a high value export product, provided the producers are forced to pay some of the profits back to the Third World countries from which they take the cane.

• . . . third world countries would become economically viable.

* . . . profitable Industrialization would be possible in Third World countries because they would have more money.

Global Economy 102

Fusion would . . .

* destroy the world market for gasoline.
* eliminate the effect of oil cartels.
* . . . oil States would suffer drastic income losses and require funds to obtain food.
* . . . desalination plants would allow irrigation of arid lands.
* . . . cheap water would allow effective agriculture world wide. Desalination plants would produce clean water at 1/20th of the cost of what the Saudis now pay for desalinated water.
* . . . these systems would stabilize the Middle-East by economic means via agriculture. Never mind idealogy. Money talks!
* . . . **this would be the biggest business in the world!**

The end-use market price of all the energy products that this end-use product would replace in a forty year replacement time is $5,000 billion a year in year 2000 dollars. $5 trillion a year . . . and lease everybody in the world to build these things . . . lease everybody . . . and charge them a royalty of 2% of gross; this would generate $100 Billion a year profit. Now that's a business!

What we need next . . .

The physics problems are gone.

We can build a demo-plant in something like 5 years. *This is something that can completely change the world!* Like the shift from wood to coal, from coal to oil, and from oil to nuclear. This is something even *more* profound than that. *It would effect every energy program on the planet once it gets going.*

This is not an attempt to *change* oil companies; it's an attempt to change the way people *live* and the way politics *works,* and the way energy is made available to human kind, and the way nations that have *nothing now* can **have** something. We think this is a good objective.

I intend that his program shall be done. If we can't do it in the United States of America, *It will be done somewhere.*

We could put enough cheap steam down the Orinoco Sand Field to get that oil out of the ground at $30 dollars a barrel, *and they have a lot* . . . seven times the oil of the Saudi's.

We may not like *Chavez,* but he's got a lot of oil.

Somebody out there will do it if *we* don't. And I think its a shame if we don't.

I came here [to Google] because of your Google mentality-set.

Maybe *you guys will do it . . .*

Thank you.

16
The New World Order

The New World Order cannot become a functional reality so long as the United States remains independent and able to go it alone. If the American people were to awaken to the realities of world politics and regain control over their government they would still have the military and economic power to break away.

Among the world planners, therefore, it has become the *prime directive* to weaken the United States both militarily and economically. And this directive has come from *American* leaders, not those of other countries.

CFR members sitting in the White House, the State Department, the Defense Department, and the Treasury are working to finalize that part of the New World Order plan. Once it gains sufficient momentum, it will pass the critical point of no return.

The IMF/World Bank is already functioning, in conjunction with the Federal Reserve System, as a world central bank. The American economy is being deliberately exhausted through foreign giveaways and domestic boondogles. The object is not to help those in need nor to preserve the environment, but to bring the system down.

When once-proud and independent Americans are standing in soup lines, they will be ready to accept the carefully arranged "rescue" by the world bank. A world currency is already designed, awaiting only an appropriate crisis to justify its introduction. From that too, there will be no escape.

The substance of these stratagems can be traced back to a 1966 think-tank study called the *Report from Iron Mountain* produced by the Hudson Institute, located at the base of Iron Mountain in Croton-on-Hudson, New York. The self-proclaimed purpose of the study was to explore various ways to "stabilize society." Praise worthy as that may sound, a reading of the *Report* reveals that the word *society* is used synonymously with the word *government,* and the word *stabilize* is used synonymously with the concept to *preserve* and *perpetuate* government. It is clear from the start that the nature of the study is to analyze the different ways a government can perpetuate itself in power, ways to control its citizens and prevent them from rebelling.

According to the *Report,* morality is not an issue. Ideology is not an issue, nor patriotism, nor religious precepts. Its sole concern is how to perpetuate the existing government. The report said:

> We have attempted to apply the standards of physical science to our thinking, the principle characteristic of which is not quantification, as is popularly believed, but that, in Whitehead's words, "...it ignores all judgments of value; for instance, all esthetic and moral judgments."[1]

The major conclusion of the report is that, in the past, war has been the only reliable means for the government to perpetuate itself in power. It contends that only during times of war or the threat of war are the masses compliant enough to carry the yoke of government without complaint. Fear of conquest and pillage by an enemy can make almost any burden seem acceptable by comparison. No amount of sacrifice in the name of victory will be rejected. Resistance is viewed as treason. In times of peace, people become resentful of high taxes and bureaucratic intervention. When they become disrespectful of their leaders, they become dangerous. No government has long survived without enemies and armed conflict. War, therefore, has been an indispensable condition for "stabilizing society." The report said:

> The war system not only has been essential to the existence of nations as independent political entities, but has been equally indispensable to their stable political structure. Without it, no government has ever been able to obtain acquiescence in its "legitimacy," or the right to rule its society. The possibility of war provides the sense of external necessity without which no government can long remain in power. It has assured the subordination of the citizens to the state. The failure of a regime to maintain the credibility of a war threat eventually leads to its dissolution, by the forces of private interest, of reactions to social injustice, or of other disintegrative elements.

The report then explains that we are approaching a point in history where the old formulas may no longer work. It may now be possible to create a world government in which all nations will be disarmed and disciplined by a world army in a condition which will be called "peace."

The report says: "The word *peace,* as we have use it, implies total and general disarmament."[2] Independent nations will no longer exist and governments will not have the capability to wage war. There could be "military actions" by the world army against political sub-divisions, but these will be *"peace-keeping operations,"* and armed soldiers will be called *"peace keepers."*

The report then raises the subject of a suitable *substitute for war.* What *else* could the world government use to *legitimate and perpetuate* itself? To provide the answer to this question was the stated purpose of the study. There can be no substitute for war unless it is (1) economically wasteful, (2) represents a credible threat of great magnitude, and (3) provides a logical excuse for compulsory service to the government, a sophisticated form of slavery.

Standing armies, or forced-labor battalions, provide a place for the government to put antisocial and dissident elements of society for serving the common good in some fashion.

The report considered ways in which the public could be preoccupied with non-important activities so that it would not have time nor the energy to participate in political debate or resistance. Recreation, trivial game shows, pornography, situation comedies . . . but games of competitive violence were considered to be the most promising. These events must evoke a passionate team loyalty on the part of the fans and must include the expectation of pain and injury on the part of the players, even better, the spilling of blood and the possibility of death. Boxing matches, football games, hockey games, and automobile races attract millions of cheering fans, like gladiator contests of old and public executions by wild beasts.

Therefore a new enemy must be found that threatens the entire world. The prospects of being overwhelmed by that enemy must be as terrifying as war itself. Allegiance requires a cause and a cause requires an enemy. Such as a war against "terrorists," against "global warming," or an "oil crisis" that simply doesn't exist.

Poverty was examined as a potential threat but rejected as being not fearful enough. Most of the world was already in poverty. Only those who have never experienced poverty would see it as a global threat. For the rest, it was simply an everyday fact of life.

The *final* candidate for a useful global threat was *pollution of the environment,* based partly on fact, and, therefore, a credible *end-of-the-earth scenario* that could be sold as just as horrible as atomic war. Accuracy in these threats would not be important. Their purpose would be to *frighten,* not inform. It might even be necessary to deliberately *manufacture* such threats by false flag crises.

The masses would more willingly accept a falling standard of living, tax increases, and bureaucratic intervention in their lives, as "the price we must pay to save Mother Earth." If a vision of destruction and death could be implanted in the public's subconscious mind, then the global battle against it could replace war as the mechanism for control.

The important point is that *The Report from Iron Mountain* explains the reality that surrounds us today. The concepts presented in it are now being implemented in almost every detail, today. Every major trend in American life is conforming to the *Iron Mountain* blueprint.

The financial crisis, the destruction of American industry, job losses, home foreclosures, wasteful spending, foreign aid, a job corp., gun control, a national police force, the apparent demise of the Soviet power, disarmament, a UN army, a world bank, a world money, ecological hysteria, and the surrender of national independence through treaties, etc.

The Report from Iron Mountain is an accurate summary of the deliberate plan that has *already* created our present, — and is now *shaping* our future.

----

1. Leonard Lewin, ed., *Report from Iron Mountain on the Possibility and Desirability of Peace,* (New York: Dell Publishing, 1967), pp. 13-14.

2. *Ibid.,* p. 9

17
U.S. Ecological Aggressor

The use of compulsion is an important point in the United Nations' plan. People in the industrialized nations are not expected to cooperate in their own demise. They will have to be forced. They will not like it when their food is taken for global distribution. They will not approve when they are taxed by a world authority to finance foreign political projects. They will not *voluntarily* give up their cars or resettle into smaller houses or communal barracks to satisfy the resource-allocation quotas of the U.N.

Club-of-Rome member Maurice Strong states the problem:

In effect, the United States is committing *environmental aggression* against the rest of the world. At the military level, the United States is the Custodian. At the environmental level, the United States is the greatest risk. One of the worst problems in the United States is energy prices — they are too low.

It is clear that the current life-styles, and consumption patterns, of the affluent middle class, involving high meat intake, consumption of large amounts of frozen and 'convenience' foods, ownership of motor-vehicles, numerous electrical appliances, home and work-place air conditioning, expansive suburban housing, are not sustainable.[1]

Maurice Strong's remarks were enthusiastically received

by world environmental leaders, but they prompted this angry editorial response in the *Arizona Republic:*

> Translated from eco-speak, this means two things: (1) a reduction in the standard of living in Western nations through massive new taxes and regulations, and (2) a wholesale transfer of wealth from industrialized to under-developed countries. The dubious premise here is that if the U.S. economy could be reduced to, say, the size of Malaysia's, the world would be a better place. Most Americans probably would balk at the idea of the U.N. banning automobiles in the U.S.[2]

Who is this Mr. Strong who sees the United States as the environmental aggressor against the world? Does he live in poverty? Does he come from a backward country that is resentful of American prosperity? Does he himself live in modest circumstances, avoiding consumption in order to preserve our natural resources? None of the above. He is one of the wealthiest men in the world. He lives and travels in great comfort. He is a lavish entertainer. In addition to having great personal wealth derived from the oil industry in Canada — which he helped nationalize — Maurice Strong was the Secretary-General of the 1992 Earth Summit in Rio; head of the 1972 UN Conference on Human Environment in Stockholm; the first Secretary-General of the UN Environment Program; president of the World Federation of United Nations; co-chairman of the World Economic Forum; member of the Club of Rome; trustee of the Aspen Institute; and a director of the World Future Society.

That is probably more than you wanted to know about this man, but it is necessary in order to appreciate the importance of what follows.

A PLOT FOR ECONOMIC CRISIS

Maurice Strong believes, or says that he believes, that the world's ecosystems can be preserved only if the affluent nations of the world can be disciplined into lowering their standard of living. Production and consumption must be curtailed. To bring that about, those nations must submit to rationing, taxation, and political domination by world government. They will probably not do that voluntarily, he says, so they will have to be forced. To accomplish this, it will be necessary to engineer a global financial crisis which will destroy their economic system. Then they will have no choice but to accept assistance and control from the UN.

This strategy was revealed in the May, 1990, issue of *West* magazine, published in Canada. In an article entitled "The Wizard of Baca Grande," journalist Daniel Wood described his week-long experience at Strong's private ranch in southern Colorado. This ranch has been visited by such CFR notables as David Rockefeller, Secretary of State Henry Kissinger, founder of the World Bank Robert McNamara, and the presidents of such organizations as IBM, Pan Am, and Harvard College.

During Wood's stay at the ranch, the Tycoon talked freely about environmentalism and politics. To express his own world views, he said he was planning to write a novel about a group of world leaders who decide to save the planet. As the plot unfolds, it becomes obvious that it is based on real people and real events.

Wood continues the story:

Each year, Strong explains as background to telling the novel's plot, the World Economic Forum convenes in Davos, Switzerland. Over a thousand CEOs, prime ministers, finance ministers, and leading academics gather at Davos in February to attend meetings and set economic agendas for the year ahead. With this as a setting, Strong then says: "What if a small group of these world leaders were to conclude that the principal risk to the earth comes from the actions of the rich countries? [*like emitting too much carbon*] And if the world is to survive, those rich countries would have to sign an agreement [*a treaty*] reducing their impact on the environment. Will they do it? The group's conclusion is 'no,' the rich countries won't do it. They won't change. So, in order "to save the planet," the group decides that the *only* hope for the planet is that the industrialized civilizations collapse. Isn't it our responsibility to bring this about?"

"This group of world leaders," Strong continues, "form a secret society to bring about an economic collapse. It's February. They're all at Davos. These Aren't terrorists. They're *world leaders.* They have positioned themselves in the world's commodity and stock markets. They've engineered, using their access to stock exchanges and computers and gold supplies, a panic. Then, they hire mercenaries who hold the rest of the world leaders at Davos as hostages. The markets *can't close.* The rich countries ..." and Strong then made a light motion with his fingers as if he were flicking a cigarette butt out the window.

I sit there spellbound. This is not just *any* story-teller talking, it is Maurice Strong. He knows these world leaders. He is, in fact, co-chairman of the Council of the World Economic Forum. He sits at the fulcrum of power. He's in a position to *do it.*

"I probably shouldn't be saying things like this," Strong says.[3]

Maurice Strong's fanciful plot probably shouldn't be taken *too* seriously, at least in terms of the *literal* reading of future events. It is unlikely they will unfold in exactly this manner, although it is not impossible. For one thing, it would not be necessary to hold the leaders of the industrialized nations at gun point. *They* would be the ones engineering this plot. Leaders from Third-World countries do not have the *means* to cause a global crisis. That would have to come from the money centers in New York, London, or Tokyo.

Furthermore, the masterminds behind this thrust for global government have always resided in the industrialized nations. They have come from the ranks of the CFR in America and from other branches of the International Roundtable in England, France, Belgium, Canada, Japan, and elsewhere. They are the ideological descendants of Cecil Rhodes and they are fulfilling his dream.

It is not important whether or not Maurice Strong's plot for global economic collapse is to be taken literally. What is important is that men like him are *thinking* along these lines. As Wood pointed out, they are in a position to *do it.* Or something *like* it. If it is not *this* scenario, they will consider *other* ones with similar consequences. If History has proven anything, it is that men with financial and political power are quite capable of heinous plots against their fellow men. They have launched wars, caused depressions, and created famines to suit their personal agendas. We have little reason to believe that the world leaders of today are more saintly than their predecessors.

Furthermore, we must not be fooled by pretended concern for Mother Earth. The call-to-arms for "saving the planet" is a gigantic *ruse.* There is just enough truth to environmental pollution to make the show "credible," as *The Report from Iron Mountain* phrases it, but the end-of-earth scenarios which drive the movement forward are bogus. The *real* objective in all of this is world government, the ultimate doomsday mechanism from which there can be no escape. Destruction of the economic strength of the industrialized nations is merely a necessary prerequisite for ensnaring them into the global web.

The thrust of the current ecology movement is directed totally to this end.

The purpose of the *Iron Mountain* study was to analyze methods by which a government can perpetuate itself in power — ways to control its citizens and prevent them from rebelling. The conclusion of the report was that, in the past, war has been the only reliable means to achieve this goal. Under world government, however, war technically would be impossible. So the main purpose of the study was to explore *other* methods for controlling populations and keeping them loyal to their leaders, and keeping their leaders in power. It was concluded that a suitable substitute for war would require a *new* enemy which poses a frightful threat to survival. Neither the threat nor the enemy has to be real. They merely have to be believable, such as the war on terrorism, or on drugs.

Oil Beneath Our Feet

Several surrogates for war were considered, but the only one that held *real* promise was the environmental-pollution model. This was viewed as the most likely to succeed because (1) it can be related to observable conditions such as smog and water pollution. In other words, it can be based partly on fact and, therefore, believable — and (2) predictions can be made showing end-of-earth scenarios just as horrible as atomic warfare. Accuracy in these predictions would not be important. Their purpose would be to *frighten people,* not to inform them.

While the *followers* of the current environmental movement are preoccupied (distracted) with visions of planetary doom, the *leaders* have an entirely *different* agenda. World Government . . . Globalism!

----

1. "Ecology Remedy Costly," (AP), *Sacramento Bee,* March 12, 1992, p. A8. Also Maurice Strong, Introduction to Jim MacNeil, Pieter Winsemius, and Taizo Yakushiji, *Beyond Interdependence* (New York: Oxford University Press, 1991), p. ix.

2. "Road to Ruin," Arizona Republic, March 26, 1992.

3. "The Wizard of Baca Grande," by Daniel Wood, *West* magazine, May, 1990.

Oil Beneath Our Feet

The Road Ahead

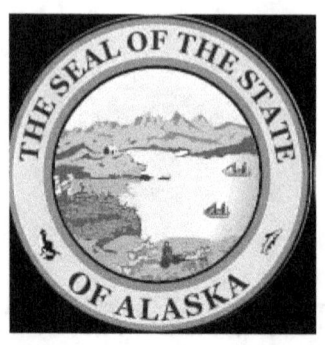

Oil Beneath Our Feet

ABOUT SARAH

Governor Sarah Palin first made history on Dec. 4, 2006. Sworn in that day as the 11th governor of Alaska, she is the first woman to hold the office. In August 2008, Senator John McCain tapped Governor Palin to serve as his vice presidential running mate in his Presidential campaign, thus making her the first woman to run on the Republican Party's presidential ticket.

In Alaska, her top priorities have been resource development, education, health, and transportation and infrastructure development. Governor Palin has fought for reform and transparency in government.

Governor Palin has a long record of achievement and experience in public office. Prior to her election as governor, Palin served two terms on the Wasilla City Council and two terms as the mayor/manager of Wasilla. During her tenure, she reduced property tax levels while increasing services and made Wasilla a business friendly environment, drawing in new industry.

Under her leadership as Governor, Alaska has invested $5 billion in state savings, overhauled education funding, and implemented the Senior Benefits Program that provides support for low-income older Alaskans. She created Alaska's Petroleum Systems Integrity Office to provide oversight and maintenance of oil and gas equipment, facilities and infrastructure, and the Climate Change Subcabinet to prepare a climate change strategy for Alaska.

During her first legislative session, Governor Palin's administration passed two major pieces of legislation - an overhaul of the state's ethics laws and a competitive process to construct a gas pipeline.

Governor Palin is past chair of the Interstate Oil and Gas Compact Commission, a multi-state government agency that promotes the conservation and efficient recovery of domestic oil and natural gas resources while protecting health, safety and the environment. She was recently named chair of the National Governors Association (NGA) Natural Resources Committee, which is charged with pursuing legislation to ensure state needs are considered as federal policy is formulated in the areas of agriculture, energy, environmental protection and natural resource management.

Sarah Heath Palin arrived in Alaska with her family in 1964, when her parents came to teach school in Skagway. She received a Bachelor of Science Degree in Communications-Journalism from the University of Idaho in 1987.

She is married to Todd Palin, who is a lifelong Alaskan, a production operator on the North Slope and a four-time champion of the Iron Dog, the world's longest snow machine race. They have five children.

America's Energy Non-Crisis!   107

Gov. Sarah Louise Palin

Oil Beneath Our Feet

18
Gov. Sarah Louise Palin

Sarah Louise Palin [Heath]; (*born February 11, 1964*) is an *American* politician who served as *Governor of Alaska* from 2006 until *she stepped down in 2009.* She was the *Republican* candidate for *Vice President of the United States* in 2008.

Sarah was a member of the *Wasilla, Alaska, city council* from 1992 to 1996 and the city's *mayor* from 1996 to 2002. After an unsuccessful campaign for *Lieutenant Governor* of Alaska in 2002, she chaired the *Alaska Oil and Gas Conservation Commission* from 2003 until her resignation in 2004. She was elected *Governor of Alaska* in November 2006. Palin became the first *female governor* of Alaska and the *youngest person* ever elected as governor of that state.

In 2008, Republican presidential candidate *John McCain* chose Sarah as his *running mate* in that year's *presidential election,* making her the *second female candidate* and the *first Alaskan candidate* of either major party on a national ticket, as well as the *first female vice-presidential nominee of the Republican Party.* Since the defeat of the McCain–Palin ticket in the 2008 election, there has been speculation that she may run for the *Republican presidential nomination* in 2012.

On July 3, 2009, Sarah announced she would not seek reelection as governor and that she was stepping down, effective July 26, 2009, eighteen months prior to the completion of her first term. She cited frivolous, *harassing ethics complaints* that had been filed following her selection as running mate to John McCain as the reason for her leaving the office of governor, saying the resulting *fruitless investigations* had affected her efficacy to govern the state.

History, Structure, Mission

The *Alaska Oil and Gas Conservation Commission* (AOGCC) is a *quasi-judicial* agency in the U.S. state of Alaska, within Alaska's *Department of Administration.* The Commission was established in 1955, was subsequently abolished, and eventually reestablished. This Commission is responsible for overseeing oil and gas drilling and production, reservoir depletion, and certain other operations on private and state-owned lands in Alaska.

A territorial statute created the *Alaska Oil and Gas Conservation Commission* (AOGCC) in 1955, before Alaska became a state in 1959. At that time, the Commission comprised the *Territorial Governor, the Commissioner of Mines,* and the *Highway Engineer.* Rules and regulations for the Commission's activities took effect in 1958.

In 1959, the *Oil and Gas Conservation Commission* was temporarily abolished, and its duties were transferred to the *Alaska Department of Natural Resources.* In 1968, the *Division of Oil and Gas* was formed within the *Department of Natural Resources.* In 1976, the word "conservation" was added back to the division's title, and it became the *Division of Oil and Gas Conservation.*

In 1977, with oil production occurring in Prudhoe Bay, the *Alaska Legislature* decided that an independent quasi-judicial agency should be created in the executive branch of the state. The present independent agency was at first located within the *Department of Natural Resources,* but in 1980 was transferred to the *Department of Commerce and Economic Development.* In 1994, it was transferred to the *Department of Administration.*

The structure of the membership has changed throughout the years, though it has consistently been a *three-member Commission.*

Under the current structure, adopted in 1979, one member must be *a registered petroleum engineer,* one member must be *a registered geologist,* and one member must *represent the public at large* (i.e., a citizen in neither of the two categories listed above).

The Commission is tasked to work *in-hand with the oil industry* to maximize production, administer correlative rights, and improve resource recovery. It also administers an *underground injection program* for enhanced oil recovery and underground disposal of oil field waste, as authorized by the U.S. Environmental Protection Agency. As part of this injection process, *oil corporations must obtain an Aquifer Exemption Order* granted by the AOGCC in areas with deep groundwater supplies. Some environmental groups such as the *Cook Inletkeeper* as well as *First Nation People* have contested these Orders, fearing they may contaminate groundwater supplies. The Commission also holds oversight of wastewater disposal known as *"wastewater drain fields,"* where as such, oil corporations are permitted to dispose of wastewater in the soil when certain requirements are met ; and reject Orders when not met. Additionally, the Commission adjudicates *certain oil and gas disputes* between owners, including *disputes where the state is a party.* It is designed to cooperate with industry, *while still meeting its regulatory requirements.* The Commission's website lists their primary mission is *"to protect the public interest in exploration and development of*

oil and gas resources, while ensuring conservation prac-
tices, enhancing resource recovery, and protecting the
health, safety, environment, and property rights of Alas-
kans." Although the *Cook Inletkeeper* website notes that
"2 billion gallons of toxic waste" are disposed of in the
Cook Inlet waterway every year by oil corporations

Early life and career

Palin was born in *Sandpoint, Idaho,* the third of four
children born to Sarah and Charles R. Heath, respectively
a school secretary and science teacher / track coach. The
family moved to Alaska when she was an infant. She attended *Wasilla High School,* where she was the head of
the *Fellowship of Christian Athletes,* and a member of the
girls' cross country team. As captain and point guard of the
school's *girls' basketball team* that won the Alaska state
championship in 1982, she gained the nickname *"Barra-*
cuda" for her competitive streak. She graduated in 1982.

She attended *Hawaii Pacific University* in the Fall of
1982 and *North Idaho College* (whose Alumni Association
gave her the *Distinguished Alumni Achievement Award* in
June 2008) in the Spring and Fall of 1983. In 1984, after
winning the *Miss Wasilla pageant,* she finished third in the
Miss Alaska pageant, receiving the *"Miss Congeniality"*
award and a college scholarship.

She attended the *University of Idaho* in the Fall of 1984
and Spring of 1985, *Matanuska-Susitna College* in the Fall
of 1985, and the *University of Idaho* again in the Spring
and Fall of 1986 and the Fall of 1987, when she received
her *Bachelor's degree in communications* with an empha-
sis in *journalism.*

Palin's early ambition was to be a *sportscaster.* Accordingly, after graduating, she worked as a *sportscaster* for

KTUU-TV and KTVA-TV in Anchorage, and as a *sports reporter* for the *Mat-Su Valley Frontiersman.* In 1988, she eloped with her childhood sweetheart *Todd Palin,* believing that her parents "couldn't afford a big white wedding." After the marriage, she helped in her husband's commercial fishing business.

Early political career
Wasilla city council

Motivated by concerns that revenue from a new *Wasilla sales tax* would not be spent wisely, Palin was elected to the *city council of Wasilla* in 1992. She won 530 (63%) votes to 310. She ran for reelection in 1995, winning by 413 (69%) votes to 185, but did not complete her second term on the city council because she was elected mayor in 1996. Throughout her tenure on the city council and the rest of her career, Palin has been a registered Republican.

Mayor of Wasilla

Palin served two three-year terms (1996–2002) as the mayor of *Wasilla.* In 1996, she defeated three-term incumbent mayor John Stein, on a platform *targeting wasteful spending and high taxes.* Stein says that Palin introduced *abortion, gun rights,* and *term limits* as campaign issues. Although the election was a *nonpartisan blanket primary,* the state Republican Party ran advertisements on her behalf. At the conclusion of Palin's tenure as mayor in 2002, the city had about 6,300 residents. In 2008, Wasilla's mayor credited Palin's tax cuts and infrastructural improvements with helping the local economy, "bringing the big-box stores to Wasilla, ... helping Wasilla grow and draw 50,000 shoppers a day." The *Boston Globe* quoted a local business owner as crediting Palin with making the town "more of a community ... It's no longer a little strip town that you can blow through in a heartbeat."

First term, *Wasilla, Alaska*

Shortly after taking office in October 1996, Palin consolidated the position of museum director and asked for updated *resumes and resignation letters* from "city department heads who had been loyal to Stein," including the police chief, public works director, finance director, and librarian. Palin stated this request was *to find out their intentions and whether they supported her.* She temporarily required department heads *to get her approval before talking to reporters,* saying that they first needed to become acquainted with her administration's policies. She created the position of city administrator, and *reduced her own $68,000 salary* by 10%, although by mid-1998 *this was reversed by the city council.*

During her first year in office, Palin kept a jar with the names of Wasilla residents on her desk. Once a week, she pulled a name from it and picked up the phone; she would ask: "How's the city doing?" Using income generated by a 2% sales tax that was enacted before she was elected to the city council, Palin *cut property taxes by 75%* and eliminated *personal property and business inventory taxes.*[Using municipal bonds, she made improvements to the roads and sewers, and increased funding to the Police Department. She also oversaw *new bike paths* and procured funding for *storm-water treatment* to protect freshwater resources. At the same time, the city reduced spending on the town museum and stopped construction of a new library and city hall.

Palin ran for re-election against Stein in 1999 and won, with 74% of the vote. She was also elected president of the *Alaska Conference of Mayors.*

Palin appointed Charles Fannon to replace Stambaugh as police chief.

Second term

During her second term as mayor, Palin introduced a *ballot measure* proposing the construction of a *municipal sports center* to be financed by a 0.5% sales tax increase. The $14.7 million *Wasilla Multi-Use Sports Complex* was built on time and under budget, but the city spent an additional $1.3 million because of an *eminent domain lawsuit* caused by the failure to obtain clear title to the property before beginning construction. The city's long-term debt grew from about $1 million to $25 million through *voter-approved indebtedness* of $15 million for the sports complex, $5.5 million for street projects, and $3 million for water improvement projects. A city council member defended the spending increases as being *caused by the city's growth* during that time.

Palin also joined with nearby communities in jointly hiring the Anchorage-based lobbying firm of *Robertson, Monagle & Eastaugh* to lobby for federal funds. The firm secured nearly $8 million in *earmarked funds* for the Wasilla city government. Earmarks included $500,000 for a *youth shelter,* $1.9 million for a *transportation hub,* and $900,000 for *sewer repairs.* Term limits in the Wasilla Municipal Code proscribe candidates from running for more than two consecutive terms.

Controversies

Wasilla librarian Mary Ellen Emmons strongly objected to remarks by Palin that Emmons characterized as being about *book censorship.* Emmons said that Palin asked two or three times in October 1996 if she would object to books being removed from the library. Palin has said the question was "rhetorical". John Stein, the former mayor of Wasilla and Palin's 1996 political opponent, said in September 2008 that Palin's *"religious beliefs"* and the concerns of some voters about language in the books, *motivated her inquiries.* In December 1996, Palin said she had no books or other material in mind for removal. No books were removed from the library, and Palin stated in 2006 that she *would not allow her personal religious beliefs* to dictate her political positions.

Police Chief Irl Stambaugh, who was eventually fired by Palin *for due cause* was previously nominated to be Alaska's Municipal Employee of the Year. Because he had heard that Palin had felt intimidated by him during a meeting, he made sure to sit when talking with her, and to use a soothing voice. Nevertheless, Palin said, *"When I met with you in private, instead of engaging in interactive conversation with me, you gave me short, uncommunicative answers and then you would sit there and stare at me in silence with a very stern look, like you were trying to intimidate me."* On January 30, Stambaugh was on the phone with the town's librarian — who said she had just been fired — when an assistant of Palin's walked up and gave Stambaugh an envelope. Inside was a letter from Palin, saying Stambaugh, too, was fired. His firing was to be effective February 13.

Palin said that she fired Emmons and Stambaugh because *they did not fully support her efforts to govern the city.* The next day, following expressions of public support for Emmons at a personal meeting, *Palin rescinded the firing of Emmons,* stating that her concerns had been alleviated, and adding that *Emmons agreed to support Palin's plan to merge the town's library and museum operations.*

Palin described the letters as just a test of loyalty. Stambaugh, who along with Emmons *had supported Palin's opponent in the election,* filed a lawsuit alleging *wrongful termination, violation of his contract,* and *gender discrimination.* In the trial, the defense alleged *political reasons;* Stambaugh said that he had opposed a gun control bill, Alaska Senate Bill 177, that Palin supported. The federal judge said in the decision that *the police chief serves at the discretion of the mayor, and can be terminated for nearly any reason, even a political one,* and dismissed Stambaugh's lawsuit ordering Stambaugh to pay Palin's legal fees.

Post-mayoral years

In 2002, Palin ran for the Republican nomination for *lieutenant governor,* coming in *second* to Loren Leman in a five-way Republican primary. The Republican ticket of U.S. Senator Frank Murkowski and Leman won the November 2002 election. When Murkowski resigned from his long-held *U.S. Senate seat* in December 2002 to become governor, he *considered* appointing Palin to replace him in the Senate, but chose his daughter, *State Representative Lisa Murkowski instead.*

Governor Murkowski appointed Palin to the *Alaska Oil and Gas Conservation Commission.* She chaired the Commission beginning in 2003, serving as *Ethics Supervisor.* Palin resigned in January 2004, protesting what she called the *"lack of ethics" of fellow Republican members.*

After resigning, Palin *filed a formal complaint against Oil and Gas Conservation Commissioner Randy Ruedrich,* also the chair of the state Republican Party, *accusing him of doing work for the party on public time and of working closely with a company he was supposed to be regulat-*

ing. She also joined with Democratic legislator Eric Croft to file a complaint against Gregg Renkes, *a former Alaskan Attorney General,* accusing him of *having a financial conflict of interest in negotiating a coal exporting trade agreement, while Renkes was the subject of investigation and after records suggesting a possible conflict of interest had been released to the public.* Ruedrich and Renkes both resigned and Ruedrich paid a record $12,000 fine.

From 2003 to June 2005, Palin served as *one of three directors* of *"Ted Stevens Excellence in Public Service, Inc.,"* a *527 group* designed to provide political training for Republican women in Alaska. In 2004, Palin told the *Anchorage Daily News* that she had decided not to run for the U.S. Senate that year, against the Republican incumbent, *Lisa Murkowski,* because her teenage son opposed it. Palin said, *"How could I be the team mom if I was a U.S. Senator?"*

Governor of Alaska

In 2006, running on a clean-government platform, Palin defeated *incumbent Governor Frank Murkowski in the Republican gubernatorial primary.* Her running mate was *State Senator Sean Parnell.* She will not be a candidate for re-election as Governor in 2010.

In the November election, Palin was *outspent but victorious,* defeating former Democratic governor Tony Knowles by a margin of 48.3% to 40.9%. She became *Alaska's first female governor,* at the age of 42, the youngest governor in Alaskan history, the state's first governor to have been born after Alaska achieved U.S. statehood, *and the first not to be inaugurated in the state capital Juneau (she chose to have the ceremony held in Fairbanks instead).*

She took office on December 4, 2006, and for most of

her term was very popular with Alaska voters. Polls taken in 2007 showed her with 93% and 89% popularity among all voters, which led *some media outlets* to call her *"the most popular governor in America."* A poll taken in late September 2008 after Palin was named to the national Republican ticket showed her popularity in Alaska at 68%. A poll taken in May 2009 showed Palin's popularity among Alaskans was at 54% positive and 41.6% negative.

Palin declared that top priorities of her administration would be *resource development, education and workforce development, public health and safety,* and *transportation and infrastructure development.* She had championed *ethics reform* throughout her election campaign. Her first legislative action after taking office was to *push for a bipartisan ethics reform bill.* She signed the resulting legislation in July 2007, calling it a "first step" *declaring that she remained determined to clean up Alaska politics.*

Palin has frequently *broken with the state Republican establishment.* For example, she endorsed Sean Parnell's bid to unseat the state's longtime at-large U.S. Representative, Don Young, and she publicly challenged then-Senator Ted Stevens *to come clean about the federal investigation into his financial dealings.* Shortly before his July 2008 indictment, she held a joint news conference with Stevens, described by *The Washington Post* as needed "to make clear she had not abandoned him politically."

Palin promoted *oil and natural gas resource development in Alaska, including drilling in the Arctic National Wildlife Refuge* (ANWR). Proposals to drill for oil in ANWR have been the subject of a *national debate.*

In 2006, Palin obtained a passport and in 2007 traveled for the first time outside of North America on a trip to Kuwait. There she visited the *Khabari Alawazem Crossing* at the Kuwait–Iraq border and met with members of the *Alaska National Guard* at several bases.[On her return trip to the U.S., *she visited injured soldiers in Germany.*

Budget, spending, and federal funds

In June 2007, Palin signed *a record $6.6 billion operating budget into law.* At the same time, she used her veto power to *make the second-largest cuts of the construction budget in state history.* The $237 million in cuts represented over 300 local projects, and *reduced the construction budget to $1.6 billion.* In 2008, Palin vetoed $286 million, *cutting or reducing funding for 350 projects* from the FY09 capital budget.

Palin followed through on a campaign promise *to sell the Westwind II jet, a purchase made by the Murkowski administration for $2.7 million in 2005 against the wishes of the legislature.* In August 2007, the jet was listed on eBay, but the sale fell through, and the plane *was later sold for $2.1 million through a private brokerage firm.*

Gubernatorial expenditures

Palin lived in Juneau during the legislative session and lived in Wasilla and worked out of offices in Anchorage the rest of the year. Since the office in Anchorage is far from Juneau, *while she worked there, state officials said she was permitted to claim a $58 per diem travel allowance, which she took* (a total of $16,951), *and reimbursements for hotels, which she refused,* choosing to drive 50 miles to her home in Wasilla instead. *She also chose not to use the former governor's private chef.*

Republicans and Democrats criticized Palin for taking the *per diem* and $43,490 in travel expenses for when her family accompanied her on state business. In response, the governor's staffers said that *these practices were in line with state policy,* that Palin's gubernatorial expenses *were 80% below those of her predecessor,* Frank Murkowski, and that *"many of the hundreds of invitations Palin receives include requests for her to bring her family, placing the definition of 'state business' with the party extending the invitation."*

In February 2009, the State of Alaska, *reversing a policy that had treated the payments as legitimate business expenses under the Internal Revenue Code,* decided that per diems paid to state employees for stays in their own homes will be treated as taxable income and will be included in employees' gross income on their W-2 forms. *Palin herself had ordered the review of the tax policy.*

In December 2008, an *Alaska State Commission* recommended increasing the Governor's annual salary from $125,000 to $150,000. *Palin stated that she would not accept the pay raise.* In response, the commission dropped the recommendation.

Federal funding

In her *State of the State Address* on January 17, 2008, Palin declared that *the people of Alaska "can and must continue to develop our economy, because we cannot and must not rely so heavily on federal government [funding]."* Alaska's federal congressional representatives cut back on *pork-barrel project requests* during Palin's time as governor; despite this, in 2008 *Alaska was still the largest per-capita recipient of federal earmarks,* requesting nearly $750 million in special federal spending over a period of two years.

While there is no sales tax or income tax in Alaska, *state revenues doubled to $10 billion in 2008.* For the 2009 budget, Palin gave a list of 31 proposed federal earmarks or requests for funding, totaling $197 million, to Alaska Senator Ted Stevens. *Palin's decreasing support for federal funding has been a leading source of friction between herself and the state's congressional delegation;* Palin has requested less in federal funding each year than her predecessor Frank Murkowski requested in his last year.

Bridge to Nowhere, *Gravina Island Bridge*

In 2005, before Palin was elected governor, Congress passed a *$442-million earmark* for constructing *two Alaska bridges* as part of an omnibus spending bill. The Gravina Island Bridge received nationwide attention as a symbol of *pork-barrel spending,* following news reports that the bridge would cost $233 million in Federal funds. Because *Gravina Island, the site of the Ketchikan airport,* has a population of 50, *the bridge became known nationally as the "Bridge to Nowhere".* Following an outcry by the public and some members of the US Senate, *Congress eliminated the bridge earmark* from the spending bill but *gave the allotted funds to Alaska as part of its general transportation fund.*

In 2006, Palin ran for governor with a *"build-the-bridge" plank* in her platform, saying she would "not allow the spinmeisters to turn this project ... into something that's so negative." Palin criticized the use of the word "nowhere" as *insulting to local residents* and urged speedy work on building the infrastructure *"while our congressional delegation is in a strong position to assist."*

As governor, Palin *canceled the Gravina Island Bridge* in September 2007, saying that Congress had *"little interest in spending any more money"* due to what she called *"inaccurate portrayals of the projects."* Alaska chose not to return the $442 million in federal transportation funds.

In 2008, as a vice-presidential candidate, *Palin characterized her position as having told Congress "thanks, but no thanks, on that bridge to nowhere."* This angered some Alaskans in Ketchikan, who said that the claim was false and a betrayal of Palin's previous support for their community. Some critics complained that this statement was misleading, since she had expressed support for the spending project and kept the Federal money after the project was canceled. *Palin received criticism for allowing construction of a 3-mile access road, built with $25 million in Federal transportation funds set aside as part of the original bridge project, to continue.* A spokesman for Alaska's Department of Transportation made a statement that it was within Palin's power to cancel the road project, but also noted that the state was still considering cheaper designs to complete the bridge project, and that in any case the road would open up the surrounding lands for development.

Gas pipeline

The Alaska gas pipeline is a proposal to transport natural gas from the <u>Alaska North Slope</u> *natural gas reserves* to the U.S. Midwest via Chicago. There are two competing projects: *one by BP and ConocoPhillips* called "Denali", and *another by <u>TransCanada Corp.</u> and <u>ExxonMobil</u>.* TransCanada has secured state seed money and a license from the state of Alaska to build and operate a pipeline, but does not yet have federal approvals needed to start construction. Denali is spending its own money to move the project forward. Both entities have said they plan to hold their respective *"open seasons"* in 2010. On June 11, 2009 TransCanada announced it had formed an agreement with

ExxonMobil to work together in bringing the gas to market.

In August 2008, Palin signed a bill authorizing the State of Alaska to award *TransCanada Pipelines*—the sole bidder to meet the state's requirements—a license to build and operate a pipeline to transport natural gas from *Alaska's North Slope* to the *Continental United States* through *Canada.* The governor also pledged $500 million in seed money to support the project. It is estimated that the project will cost $26 billion. *Newsweek* described the project as *"the principal achievement of Sarah Palin's term as Alaska's governor."* The pipeline faces legal challenges from Canadian *First Nations*.

Predator control

In 2007, Palin supported a 2003 *Alaska Department of Fish and Game* policy allowing the *hunting of wolves from the air* as part of a predator control program intended to *increase moose and caribou populations for subsistence-food gatherers and other hunters.* In March 2007, Palin's office announced that a *bounty of $150 per wolf would be paid to the 180 volunteer pilots and gunners, to offset fuel costs, in five areas of Alaska.* Six-hundred-and-seven wolves had been killed in the prior four years. State biologists wanted 382 to 664 wolves killed by the end of the predator-control season in April 2007. Wildlife activists sued the state, *and a state judge declared the bounty illegal* on the basis that a bounty would have to be offered by the Board of Game and not by the Department of Fish and Game.

Public Safety Commissioner dismissal

Palin dismissed Public Safety Commissioner Walt Monegan on July 11, 2008, citing *performance-related issues, such as not being "a team player on budgeting is-*

sues" and "egregious rogue behavior." Palin attorney Van Flein said that the "last straw" was Monegan's *planned trip to Washington, D.C., to seek funding for a new, multimillion-dollar sexual assault initiative* the governor hadn't yet approved. Monegan said that he had resisted persistent pressure from the Governor, her husband, and her staff, including State Attorney General Talis Colberg, *to fire Palin's ex-brother-in-law, state trooper Mike Wooten;* Wooten was involved in a child custody battle with Palin's sister after a bitter divorce that included *an alleged <u>death threat</u> against Palin's father.* At one point Sarah and Todd Palin hired a private investigator to get Wooten disciplined. Monegan stated that he learned *an internal investigation had found all but two of the allegations to be unsubstantiated,* and Wooten had been disciplined for the others—*an illegal moose killing and the <u>tasering</u> of an 11-year-old* (the child asked to be Tasered?). He told the Palins that there was nothing he could do because the matter was closed. When contacted by the press for comment, Monegan first *acknowledged pressure to fire Wooten but said that he could not be certain that his own firing was connected to that issue;* he later asserted that *the dispute over Wooten was a major reason for his firing.* Palin stated on July 17 that *Monegan was not pressured to fire Wooten, nor dismissed for not doing so.*

Monegan said the subject of Wooten came up when he invited Palin to a birthday party for his cousin, state senator Lyman Hoffman, in February 2007 during the legislative session in Juneau. *"As we were walking down the stairs in the capitol building she wanted to talk to me about her former brother-in-law,"* Monegan said. *"I said, 'Ma'am, I need to keep you at arm's length with this. I can't deal* about him with you." "She said, 'OK, that's a good idea.'"

Governor Palin said there was *"absolutely no pressure ever put on Commissioner Monegan to hire or fire anybody, at any time. I did not abuse my office powers. And I don't know how to be more blunt and candid and honest, but to tell you that truth. To tell you that no pressure was ever put on anybody to fire anybody."* "Never putting any pressure on him," added Todd Palin. But on August 13 she acknowledged that *a half dozen members of her administration had made more than two dozen calls on the matter to various state officials. "I do now have to tell Alaskans that such pressure could have been perceived to exist, although I have only now become aware of it,"* she said. Palin said, *"Many of these inquiries were completely appropriate. However, the serial nature of the contacts could be perceived as some kind of pressure, presumably at my direction."*

Chuck Kopp, who Palin had appointed to replace Monegan as public safety commissioner, *received a $10,000 state severance package after he resigned following just two weeks on the job.* Kopp, *the former Kenai chief of police,* resigned July 25 *following disclosure of a 2005 sexual harassment complaint and letter of reprimand against him.* Monegan said that he didn't get any severance package from the state.

Legislative investigation

On August 1, 2008 the *Alaska Legislature* hired an investigator, Stephen Branchflower, to review the Monegan dismissal. Legislators stated that *Palin had the legal authority to fire Monegan,* but they wanted to know *whether her action had been motivated by anger at Monegan for not firing Wooten.* The atmosphere was bipartisan *and*

Palin pledged to cooperate. Wooten remained employed as a state trooper. *She placed an aide on paid leave due to one tape-recorded phone conversation that she deemed improper,* in which the aide appeared to be acting on her behalf and complained to a trooper that Wooten had not been fired.

Several weeks *after the start of what the media referred to as "troopergate",* Palin was chosen as John McCain's running mate. On September 1, Palin asked the legislature to drop its investigation, saying that the state Personnel Board had jurisdiction over ethics issues. The Personnel Board's three members were first appointed by Palin's predecessor, and Palin reappointed one member in 2008. On September 19, the *Governor's husband and several state employees* refused to honor subpoenas, the validity of which were disputed by *Talis Colberg, Palin's appointee as Alaska's Attorney General.* On October 2, *a court rejected Colberg's challenge to the subpoenas,* and seven of the witnesses, not including Sarah and Todd Palin, eventually testified.

Branchflower Report

On October 10, 2008, the *Alaska Legislative Council* unanimously voted *to release, without endorsing,_the Branchflower Report,* in which investigator Stephen Branchflower found that *firing Monegan "was a proper and lawful exercise of her constitutional and statutory authority,"* but that Palin abused her power as governor and violated the state's Executive Branch Ethics Act *when her office pressured Monegan to fire Wooten .* The report stated that *"Governor Palin knowingly permitted a situation to continue where impermissible pressure was placed on several subordinates to advance a personal agenda,* to wit: to get Trooper Michael Wooten fired." The report also said that Palin "permitted Todd Palin to use the Governor's office [...] to continue to contact subordinate state employees in an effort to find some way to get Trooper Wooten fired."

On October 11, Palin's attorneys responded, condemning the Branchflower Report as "misleading and wrong on the law". One of Palin's attorneys, Thomas Van Flein, said that the Branchflower Report was an attempt to "smear the governor by innuendo." Later that day, Governor Palin did a conference call interview with various Alaskan reporters, where she stated, "Well, I'm very, very pleased to be cleared of any legal wrongdoing... Any hint of any kind of unethical activity there. Very pleased to be cleared of any of that."

State Personnel Board investigation

The State Personnel Board (SPB) reviewed the matter at Palin's request. On September 15, the Anchorage law firm of Clapp, Peterson, Van Flein, Tiemessen & Thorsness filed arguments of "no probable cause" with the SPB on behalf of Palin. The SPB hired independent counsel Timothy Petumenos as an investigator. On October 24, Palin gave three hours of depositions with the Board in St. Louis, Missouri. On November 3, Petumenos found that there was no probable cause to believe Palin or any other state official had violated state ethical standards.

Resignation

A crowd estimated at 5,000 people gathered in Fairbanks' Pioneer Park to watch Palin turn over her office to Sean Parnell.

On July 3, 2009, Palin announced at a press conference that she would not run for reelection in the 2010 Alaska *gubernatorial election and would resign before the end of July.* Palin gave a speech offering reasons for her departure. She argued that *both she and the state have been expending an "insane" amount of time and money to address "frivolous" ethics complaints filed against her.* She also said that her decision not to seek reelection *would make her a lame duck governor.* Palin did not take questions at the press conference. A Palin aide was quoted as saying *Palin was "no longer able to do the job she had been elected to do. Essentially, the taxpayers were paying for Sarah to go to work every day and defend herself."*

2008 vice-presidential campaign

On August 24, 2008, during a general strategy meeting at the *Phoenix Ritz-Carlton* with Steve Schmidt and a few other senior advisers to the *McCain Campaign,* potential vice presidential picks were discussed. Consensus began to settle around Palin; the following day, the strategists advised McCain of their conclusions and *McCain personally called Palin who was at the Alaska State Fair.*

On August 27, she visited McCain's vacation home near *Sedona, Arizona,* where she was offered the position of vice-presidential candidate. Palin was the *only prospective running mate who had a face-to-face interview with McCain to discuss joining the ticket that week.* Nonetheless, *Palin's selection was a surprise to many as speculation had centered on other candidates,* such as *Minnesota Governor* Tim Pawlenty, *Louisiana Governor* Bobby Jindal, *former Massachusetts Governor* Mitt Romney, *United States Senator* Joe Lieberman *of Connecticut,* and *former Pennsylvania Governor* Tom Ridge.

On August 29, in Dayton, Ohio, *Republican presidential candidate John McCain* announced that *he had chosen*

Palin as his running mate. According to Jill Hazelbaker, a spokeswoman for John McCain, *he first met Palin at the National Governors Association meeting in Washington in February 2008 and came away "extraordinarily impressed."*

Palin is the *first Alaskan* and the *second woman* to run on a major U.S. party ticket. The first woman was Geraldine Ferraro, the Democratic vice-presidential nominee in 1984, who ran with former vice-president Walter Mondale. On September 3, 2008, *Palin delivered a 40-minute acceptance speech at the Republican National Convention that was well-received and watched by more than 40 million viewers.*

Several conservative commentators met Palin in the summer of 2007. Some of them, such as Bill Kristol, urged McCain to pick Palin, arguing that *her presence on the ticket* would provide a boost in enthusiasm among the religious right wing of the Republican party, while *her status as an unknown on the national scene* would also be a positive factor for McCain's campaign.

Since Palin was *largely unknown outside Alaska* before her selection by McCain, her personal life, positions, and political record *drew intense media attention and scrutiny.* On September 1, 2008, *Palin announced that her daughter Bristol was pregnant and that she would marry the father, a young man named Levi.* During this period, some Republicans felt that Palin was being subjected to unreasonable media coverage, a sentiment Palin noted in her acceptance speech. A poll taken immediately after the Republican convention found that *more than half of Americans believed that the media was "trying to hurt" Palin with negative coverage.*

During the campaign, controversy erupted over alleged differences between Palin's positions as a gubernatorial candidate and her position as a vice-presidential candidate. After McCain announced Palin as his running mate, *Newsweek* and *Time* put Palin on their magazine covers, as some of the media alleged that McCain's campaign was restricting press access to Palin by allowing only three one-on-one interviews and no press conferences with her. Palin's first major interview, *with Charles Gibson of ABC News,* met with mixed reviews. Her interview five days later with *Fox News's Sean Hannity* focused on many of the same questions from Gibson's interview. *Palin's performance in her third interview, with Katie Couric of CBS News, was widely criticized;* her poll numbers declined, Republicans expressed concern that she was becoming a political liability, and some conservative commentators called for Palin to resign from the Presidential ticket. Other conservatives remained ardent in their support for Palin, accusing the columnists of elitism. Following this interview, some Republicans, *including Mitt Romney and Bill Kristol,* questioned the McCain campaign's strategy of *sheltering Palin from unscripted encounters with the press.*

Palin was reported to have prepared intensively for the October 2 *vice-presidential debate* with Democratic vice-presidential nominee Joe Biden *at Washington University in St. Louis.* Some Republicans suggested that Palin's performance in the interviews would improve public perceptions of her debate performance by lowering expectations. Polling from CNN, Fox and CBS found that *while Palin exceeded most voters' expectations, they felt that Biden had won the debate.*

Upon returning to the campaign trail after her debate

preparation, *Palin stepped up her attacks on the Democratic candidate for President, Senator Barack Obama.* At a fundraising event, Palin explained her new aggressiveness, saying, *"There does come a time when you have to take the gloves off and that time is right now."*

Palin appeared on the television show *Saturday Night Live* on October 18. *Prior to her appearance on the show, she had been parodied several times by Tina Fey,* who was noted for her physical resemblance to the candidate. In the weeks leading up to the election, Palin had also been the subject of numerous other parodies.

The election took place on November 4, and *Obama was projected as the winner at 11:00 PM Eastern Standard Time.* In his concession speech McCain thanked Palin, calling her *"one of the best campaigners I've ever seen, and an impressive new voice in our party for reform and the principles that have always been our greatest strength."* While aides were preparing the teleprompter for McCain's speech, *they found a concession speech written for Palin by Bush speechwriter Matthew Scully.* Two members of McCain's staff, Steve Schmidt and Mark Salter, told Palin that *there was no tradition of Election Night speeches by running mates,* and that she would not be speaking. *Palin appealed to McCain, who agreed with his staff.*

After the 2008 election

Palin was selected as one of America's *"Top 10 Most Fascinating People"* of 2008 for a Barbara Walters ABC special on December 4, 2008. She was the first guest on *commentator Glenn Beck's Fox News television show* on January 19, 2009, commenting on President Barack Obama that he was her president and that she would assist in any way to bring progress to the nation without abandoning her conservative views.

On January 27, 2009, Palin formed the *political action committee, SarahPAC*. The organization which describes itself as *an advocate of "energy independence,"* supports candidates for federal and state office. Following her resignation as Governor, Palin announced her intention *to campaign "on behalf of candidates who believe in the right things, regardless of their party label or affiliation."* It was reported that *SarahPAC* had raised nearly $1,000,000 by July 13, 2009, and that *only 28 of the 709 donations over $200 had come from Alaska residents.* A legal defense fund has also been set up to help Gov. Palin challenge ethics complaints, and it had collected approximately $250,000 as of mid July 2009.

Going Rogue

In November 2009, Palin released *Going Rogue: An American Life*, which quickly became a bestseller. Palin made a number of media appearances to promote the book, including a widely publicized interview on November 16, 2009 with Oprah Winfrey.

Going Rogue: An American Life is the *New York Times #1 best seller by former American Vice Presidential candidate Sarah Palin,* co-written by Lynn Vincent of San Diego, and edited by Adam Bellow for HarperCollins. The *memoir* was released on November 17, 2009, and became *the third political memoir in history to sell more than 1 million copies.* The book's title is a reference to a phrase that arose during the latter part of the *2008 presidential campaign.* Palin embraced it after the question, *"Has Sarah Palin 'gone rogue'?",* appeared in the lead of an article in the magazine, *Slate.* The subtitle, *"An American Life",* is the same as that of Ronald Reagan's 1990 autobiography.

2012 speculation

Palin's high profile in the 2008 presidential campaign fueled speculation that *she may run for the Republican presidential nomination in 2012,* and as of November 2008, there is an active *"Draft Palin" movement.* In December 2008, she campaigned for Sen. Saxby Chambliss of Georgia in his bid to be re-elected to the Senate in the run-off election. Chambliss went on to win by a larger than expected margin, and he credited Palin with *drumming up support from the conservative base of the Republican Party.* This fueled mounting speculation that Palin may run for president herself in 2012.

On the question of seeking the Presidency, Palin told CNN that, *"right now I cannot even imagine running for national office in 2012."* She has, *however,* left the door open for a future presidential run, whether it be in 2012 or at a later date.

A few polls were taken after the 2008 election on the subject of Palin's future as a presidential candidate. At the *Conservative Political Action Conference* in February 2009, a straw poll was held to determine who conservatives would be most likely to support for president in 2012. *Palin came in third, with 13%, tying Texas Congressman Ron Paul.* Former Massachusetts Governor Mitt Romney came in first with 20%, followed by Louisiana Governor Bobby Jindal with 14%. A June 2009 *CNN/Opinion Research Corporation* national poll *showed Palin as the 2012 presidential co-favorite of the Republican electorate along with Romney and Mike Huckabee.* The same month, a *Pew Research Center poll* found that *equal amounts of the general public viewed Palin favorably versus unfavorably,* with few having no opinion. This was roughly consistent with her ratings during the vice-presidential campaign. Among Republicans, however, her favorability ratings were very high, and greater than those for several other Republican political figures.

Family and religion

Palin describes herself as a *hockey mom.* The Palins have five children: sons Track (b. 1989) and Trig Paxson Van (b. 2008), and daughters Bristol Sheeran Marie (b. 1990), Willow (b. 1995), and Piper (b. 2001). Track enlisted in the U.S. Army on September 11, 2007, and was subsequently assigned to an infantry brigade. He and his unit deployed to Iraq in September 2008 for 12 months. Palin's youngest child, Trig, was prenatally diagnosed with Down syndrome. Palin has one grandchild, a boy named Tripp Easton Mitchell Johnston, who was born to her eldest daughter Bristol, in 2008. Sarah's husband Todd works for the British oil company BP as an oil-field production operator and owns a commercial fishing business.

Palin was born into a Roman Catholic family. Later, her family joined the *Wasilla Assembly of God, a Pentecostal church,* which she attended until 2002. Palin then switched to the *Wasilla Bible Church* because, she said, *she preferred the children's ministries offered there.* When in Juneau, she attends the *Juneau Christian Center.* Palin described herself in an interview as a *"Bible-believing Christian."* After the *Republican National Convention,* a spokesperson for the McCain campaign told CNN that *Palin "doesn't consider herself Pentecostal"* and *has "deep religious convictions."*

In keeping with her religious background, *Palin talked in a PBS interview of how her favorite writer is C. S. Lewis.*

Political positions

Palin has been a registered Republican since 1982, and has described the Republican Party platform as *"the right agenda for America."*

Palin is a *social conservative.*

Palin opposes *same-sex marriage.*

Palin opposes *embryonic stem cell research,* and abortion, calling herself "as *pro-life* as any candidate can be." She has referred to *abortion* as an "atrocity," but opposes sanctions against women who obtain an abortion. She supports laws requiring *parental consent* for minors seeking an abortion.

Palin supports allowing the discussion of *creationism* in public schools, but is not in favor of teaching it as part of the curriculum. She supports sex education in public schools that *encourages abstinence* but also *discusses birth control.*

A lifetime member of the *National Rifle Association* (NRA), Palin believes the *right to bear arms* includes handgun possession, is *against a ban on semi-automatic assault weapons,* and supports *gun safety education for youth.*

Palin supports *capital punishment for adults who murder children and other innocent people.*

Palin has promoted oil and natural gas resource exploration in Alaska, including in the *Arctic National Wildlife Refuge* (ANWR).

Palin has expressed skepticism about the *causes of global warming,* but agrees that "man's activities certainly can be contributing to the issue" *and that action should be taken.*

Palin is opposed to *cap-and-trade proposals* such as

the *American Clean Energy and Security Act.*

On *foreign policy,* Palin supported the Bush Administration's policies in Iraq, but is concerned that *"dependence on foreign energy"* may be obstructing efforts to *"have an exit plan in place."*

Palin supports *preemptive military action* in the face of an imminent threat, and supports U.S. military operations in Pakistan.

Palin supports *NATO membership for Ukraine and Georgia,* and affirms that if Russia invaded a NATO member, the United States *should meet its treaty obligations.*

Palin has been an outspoken opponent of *Congress' plans for health care reform,* claiming it would include *what she called "death panels,"* which would threaten handicapped people such as her son Trig.

Palin opposed *end-of-life advance directives* mentioned in page 425 of a health care bill.

Palin *declared April 16 2008 Healthcare Decisions Day* in part so that *"more citizens will execute advance directives."*

Public image

During the campaign, *Palin evoked a more strongly divided response than Joe Biden* among voters. A plurality of the television audience rated Biden's performance higher at *the 2008 vice-presidential debate.*

Media outlets repeated Palin's statement that *she "stood up to Big Oil"* when she resigned *after 11 months as the head of the Alaska Oil and Gas Conservation Commission, due to abuses she witnessed involving other Republican commissioners and their ties to energy companies and energy lobbyists,* and again when she *raised taxes on oil companies as governor.*

Others have said that Palin is a *"friend of Big Oil"* due to her advocacy of oil exploration and development including drilling in the *Arctic National Wildlife Refuge* (ANWR) and the *de-listing of the polar bear as an endangered species.* The *National Organization for Women,* which endorsed Obama, made clear that *it would not support Palin,* and made its support for her opponent publicly known. The *National Rifle Association* said nothing specific about *Palin's position on gun legislation,* but concluded that *she would be "one of the most pro-gun vice-presidents in American history."*

Following the presidential election, 69% of Republicans felt Palin had helped John McCain's bid, while 20% felt Palin hurt. In the same poll, 71% of Republicans stated Palin had been the right choice. An article by *Robert Jones & Daniel Cox, "Beyond the Spin",* in *Religion Dispatches*, uses a *"post-election" survey* to show that *McCain's choice of Palin split likely Republican voters.* She scored *highly* with White evangelicals but lost support for McCain *among White Roman Catholics.*

19
Governor Palin on Environment

Opposed protections for salmon from mining contamination

This month, Ms. Palin issued a last-minute statement of opposition to a ballot measure that would have provided added protections for salmon from potential contamination from mining, an action seen as crucial to its defeat.

Source: New York Times, pp. A1 & A10, "An Outsider Who Charms" Aug 29, 2008

Sue US government to stop listing polar bear as endangered

Governor Sarah Palin announced today the State of Alaska has filed a lawsuit in U.S. District Court for the District of Columbia seeking to overturn Interior Secretary Dirk Kempthorne's decision to list the polar bear as threatened under the Endangered Species Act.

This action follows written notice given more than 60 days ago, asking that the regulation listing the polar bear as threatened be withdrawn. "We believe that the Service's decision to list the polar bear was not based on the best scientific and commercial data available," Governor Palin said.

The Service's analysis failed to adequately consider the polar bears' survival through prior warming periods, and its findings that the polar bear is threatened by sea-ice habitat loss are not warranted. The Service also failed to adequately consider the existing regulatory mechanisms which have resulted in a sustainable worldwide polar bear population that has more than doubled in number over the last 40 years to 20,000-25,000 bears.

Source: Alaska Governor's Office: press release, "Polar Bear" Aug 4, 2008

We must encourage timber, mining, drilling, & fishing

Industry knows we want responsible development. Anadarko will drill Alaska's first-ever gas-targeted wells on the North Slope. Chevron, FEX, Renaissance—many others are exploring. That's ratification of AGIA's promise to make investments profitable for industrious explorers. There's more we can do to ramp up development. Our new reservoir study can increase development and we will ensure better, publicly supported project coordination. To cultivate timber and agriculture, we're encouraging responsible, economic efforts to revitalize our once-robust industries. We can and must continue to develop our economy, because we cannot and must not rely so heavily on federal government earmarks.

Source: 2008 State of the State Address to 25th Alaska Legislature Jan 15, 2008

Wolf predator control is important for subsistence hunters

Gov. Palin criticized Congressman George Miller's (D-CA) legislation to eliminate an important element of wildlife management by the State of Alaska. "Moose & caribou are important food for Alaskans, & Rep. Miller's bill threatens that food supply," said Gov. Palin. "Rep. Miller doesn't understand rural Alaska, doesn't comprehend wildlife management in the North, and doesn't appreciate the Tenth Amendment that gives states the right to manage their own affairs."

Miller's bill would ban the shooting of wolves from aircraft, a component of moose and caribou management plans in five specific areas of Alaska. Contrary to what Rep. Miller said in Washington yesterday, there is no "aerial hunting" of wolves in Alaska, Palin said. "Our science-driven and abundance-based predator management program involves volunteers who are permitted to use aircraft to kill some predators where we are trying to increase opportunities for Alaskans to put healthy food on their families' dinner tables. It is not hunting."

Source: <u>Alaska Governor's Office: Press release 07-197, "Wildlife"</u> Sep 26, 2007

Feds shouldn't list beluga whales as endangered

Gov. Palin has told the federal government that the state is extremely concerned about a proposal to list Cook Inlet beluga whales as an endangered species, and urged the National Marine Fisheries Service (NMFS) not to list the species.

"Our scientist feel confident that it would be unwarranted to list Cook Inlet belugas now," Gov. Palin said. "Seven years ago, NMFS determined that these whales weren't endangered, and since then, we've actually seen the beginnings of an increase in their population. We are all doing everything we can to help protect these important marine mammals."

The state submitted 95 pages of data and formal comments to NMFS on the proposed listing, pointing out that the Cook Inlet stock of belugas is recovering from an "unsustainable harvest" in the early 1990s. "I am especially concerned that an unnecessary federal listing and designation of critical habitat would do serious long-term damage to the vibrant economy of the Cook Inlet area," Palin said.

Source: Alaska Governor's Office: Press release 07-175, "Beluga" Aug 7, 2007

Provide stability in regulations for developers

I'm keenly aware of sharply declining production from North Slope fields. The amount of oil currently flowing through the Pipeline is less than half of what it was at its peak. We must look to responsible development throughout the state—from the Slope all the way down to Southeast—every region participating! From further oil and gas development, to fishing, mining, timber, and tourism, these developments remain the core of our state. We provide stability in regulations for our developers.

Source: 2007 State of the State Address to 24th Alaska Legislature Jan 17, 2007

Convince the rest of the nation to open ANWR

The standard should be no different for industry. Ironically, we're trying to convince the rest of the nation to open ANWR, but we can't even get our own Pt. Thomson, which is right on the edge of ANWR, developed! We are ready for that gas to be tapped so we can fill a natural gas pipeline. I promise to vigorously defend Alaska's rights, as resource owners, to develop and receive appropriate value for our resources.

Source: 2007 State of the State Address to 24th Alaska Legislature Jan 17, 2007

Fish platform: "Resource First" philosophy

COMMERCIAL FISHING: Fish Platform: Do What's Right For Alaska's Fishing Communities

- "Resource First" Philosophy
- Professional ADF&G Management with Adequate Funding
- Fishery Advisor
- · Balanced Board and Council Appointments
- Aggressive Marketing Campaign
- No Fish Farming allowed

I am not only a champion for Alaska's fishing industry, but I am a part of it. My family is proud to be a Bristol Bay fishing family. If we manage for abundance, we should have enough fish for all our needs.

Source: Palin-Parnell campaign booklet: New Energy for Alaska Nov 3, 2006

Rail provides critical link for business development

- The railroad provides a critical link to Interior Alaska for hauling equipment & materials, as well as passengers.
- Rail service & use has improved greatly over the past few years. The system is being managed, maintained, and upgraded to better standards.
- Rail development is ideal for transport of heavy items. If it is economically beneficial over the long term, rail should be utilized open up those areas of Alaska currently not served by roads in order to support business development.

Source: Palin-Parnell campaign booklet: New Energy for Alaska Nov 3, 2006

Supports "Roads to Resources": subsidized access to mines

When it comes to spending state money, Palin is generally conservative. Yet Palin supports the state's *roads to resources program,* which funds roads to mines and other natural resources projects such as oil and gas.

Source: Anchorage Daily News: 2006 gubernatorial candidate profile Oct 31, 2006

Don't duplicate effort in monitoring cruise ship emissions

Palin questioned environmental aspects of the new cruise ship law in an Oct. 17 letter to the Alaska Travel Industry Association, the state's major tourism group. Palin questioned whether the new environmental monitoring is "redundant" under state law and she said no other Alaska business faces the consumer disclosures now required for cruise lines. Palin worried about the law's environmental enforcement and its requirement for cruise lines to disclose their commissions for channeling passengers to flightseeing companies, rafting businesses, gift shops and other on-shore vendors.

The state Departments of Environmental Conservation and state Department of Revenue are now writing the regulations to enforce the taxes, environmental permits and disclosure rules. The new taxes and rules go into effect Dec. 17.

Source: <u>Anchorage Daily News: 2006 gubernatorial candidate profile</u> Oct 30, 2006

Don't amend AK constitution for rural subsistence

20
Sarah Palin Memoirs
Highlights from "Going Rogue"

This chapter is a compilation of Sarah Palin's statements extracted from her book, *"Going Rogue: An American Life."*

— — —

By the time I was thirty-eight, my second term [as mayor] was winding down and I was about to be term-limited out of office. Meanwhile, several people approached me saying they hoped I'd stay in public service. Not politicos, just ordinary people.

As president of the Conference of Mayors, I saw so many needs around the state, places where I felt I could help. But I had no interest in running for the state legislature. I did not think I would do well in a place where you had to scratch disagreeable backs in order to secure a nameplate in the caucus.

— — —

Having advocated for local control across the state as president of the Alaska Conference of Mayors, I added that principle to my campaign platform. I had great respect for the need for state government to preserve locally enacted policies. Likewise, I believed that national leaders have a responsibility to respect the Tenth Amendment and keep their hands off the states. It's the old Jeffersonian view that the affairs of the citizens are best left in their own hands.

— — —

I guess Murkowski took me seriously when I said my most important issues were energy and resource development. A couple of months into his administration, he offered me a job as chairman of the **Alaska Oil and Gas Conservation Commission (AOGCC)**. It was confirmation that having lost out on the lieutenant governor's position and the U.S. Senate appointment were actually blessings.

More than 85% of the state's budget is built on petroleum-based energy revenues. For more than thirty years the big oil companies like British Petroleum (BP), ExxonMobile, and ConocoPhillips have extracted the oil underneath Alaska lands and sold billions of barrels of it to very hungry markets. But oil is not a renewable resource. Once it's gone, it's gone, so it has to be dealt with prudently.

Many Alaskans were aware that these huge multinational energy corporations had been leasing oil-rich chunks of land on the North Slope, but were just sitting on the leases, in some cases for decades. And as long as they held the leases, other companies couldn't come in and compete for the right to tap our resources, so parts of the oil basis were essentially locked up.

— — —

I finally decided to toss my hat in the ring to replace Frank Murkowski as governor, and I was having a ball working long, intense days. By the end of that summer, the bottom line for me was clear: voters wanted change, and they should have a straightforward choice about what kind of change it would be. As always, Todd supported me and encouraged me to do it. So on Alaska Day, October 18, 2005, I kicked off the gubernatorial campaign with about fifty friends, family, and reporters in my living room. It was also Bristol's fifteenth birthday, so of course, we had cake.

— — —

Our campaign would focus on cleaning house in government and facilitating the private-sector development of energy resources, specifically ramping up production of America's energy supplies and building the 3,000-mile, $40 billion natural gas pipeline that other administrations had been promising to build for decodes. It would ultimately go from the North Slope to hungry Midwest markets out of a Chicago hub. I was determined that Alaska was going to start contributing more to the nation.

— — —

I would gather the information I needed and base my decisions on principle and sound ideas, not cronyism or political expediency. I ran on my record as an executive and told Alaska voters that I would govern according to conservative principles, and if I were to err, would be on the side of those principles. Like stars in the northern sky, Alaska has hundreds of tiny town and villages flung across it, and the people who live in them are the state's heart and soul. When we visited, sometimes whole towns turned out, from little kids to Native elders bearing **akutaq** [*eskimo ice cream*] and blueberry muffins and salmon strips.

— — —

Triumph on November 7, 2006!

On election night, hundreds of us filed into a ballroom at the Hotel Captain Cook to celebrate our victory. We were so thrilled and thankful — and finally tired — as the results poured in. We won with nearly half the vote in a six-way race.

— — —

All through Alaska's history, the inaugural swearing in had taken place in the capital city of Juneau. But in a break with tradition, I selected Fairbanks, the Golden Heart City, as the location for the December 4, ceremony. The fiftieth anniversary of statehood would take place during our term, so we wanted to celebrate the Alaska Constitution, which was written in Fairbanks. That was what I wanted to honor that day. Thanks to our state's simple and concise founding documents, our founding mothers and fathers had provided a level of opportunity and prosperity that other states, even other countries, could only dream of. I believed then — and still do now — that in addition to God's grace, the credit for Alaska's prosperity should be given to our Constitution's framers.

— — —

To kick off the Palin-Parnell agenda, we started with the natural gas pipeline on our first day in office.

For Alaskans, the term "gasline" is as familiar as "irrigation" is to Californians or "Wall Street" is to New Yorkers. Except that Californians and New Yorkers already reap the benefits of these economic lifelines, while Alaskans have been waiting more than fifty years to realize the benefits of the state's vast reserves of natural gas. At least 35 trillion cubic feet of proven natural gas reserves lie untapped on the North Slope, and geologists say there are hundreds of trillions more, both on- *and* offshore.

Construction of a gas pipeline to transport this safe, clean energy supply to the Lower 48 was originally authorized by the **Federal Energy Regulatory Commission (FERC)** in 1979. At the time, a lot of folks had high hopes. Not only would the pipeline become a second economic pillar of the state creating jobs and development opportunities, but it would reduce our dependence on foreign supplies and therefore our reliance on unfriendly nations,

Cheap natural gas from other countries had delayed the project for years. And for years the big producers who held leases on the gas fields sat on their contracts, preferring instead to develop projects in countries with fewer labor and environmental restrictions. It was unfortunate that our government's well-meaning policies had driven producers to other parts of the world where there were no restraints on their activities. That was no way to protect the environment or heal the economy.

With my background, I understood the concerns of all the parties: as a free-market capitalist I understood the bottom line for the oil producers; as the spouse of an oil worker I understood the Slopers and their families' reliance on oil jobs; as a mayor I understood the communities' dependence on oil's economic contributions; as a lover of the land I understood as well the environmentalists' and Alaska Natives' concerns.

Any corporate CEO is tasked with looking out for the

bottom line. Our state Constitution stipulates that the citizens *actually own* our natural resources. Oil companies would partner with Alaskans to develop our resources, and the corporations would make decisions based on the best interests of their shareholders, and that was fine. But in fulfillment of my oath, I would make decisions based on the best interests of *our* shareholders, the people of Alaska.

So in my Anchorage office, we established the ground rules for the gasline team. Our goal was to commercialize Alaska's treasure of oil and gas by opening up the North Slope basin to long-term exploration and production, thus creating jobs and ensuring a stable energy supply.

— — —

Under Murkowski's administration, gasline renegotiation had taken place behind closed doors.

My friend Tom had told Murkowski one too many times that the secret gasline deal he was negotiating with ExxonMobile, BP, and ConocoPhillips violated the state's Constitution. Among other things, his approach reliquished state sovereignty, and would unwisely lock in tax rates for decades into the future despite volatility in the markets.

So I put my name and commitment behind a proposal to open bidding to the private sector.

Our approach to moving the gasline forward was both innovative and simple: Explain the importance of gasline development to ordinary Alaskans. And get them involved. That meant our war room became every kitchen table, town hall, classroom, and living room across the Last Frontier.

We reached out. We asked citizens. "These are your

resources, so what do *you* think?"

Internally, our natural gas mantra was *"Greenies, Grannies, and Gunnies."*

Greenies: natural gas is the cleanest nonrenewable fuel.

Grannies: production of a domestic supply from Alaska would help those on fixed incomes, such as the elderly, by increasing supply and lowering costs in a more stable price environment.

Gunnies: Alaska's energy supplies would help lead America toward energy independence and greater national security.

Greenies, Grannies, and Gunnies. So Alaskan. So politically incorrect. Perfect.

— — —

The size of Alaska is difficult to comprehend for anyone living in the Lower 48. It is huge, one-fifth the size of the entire continental U.S. When the kids and I moved to Juneau in January 2007, Todd and I worked more than 1,300 miles apart. Adding to the challenge, you can't drive between Prudhoe Bay and our capital city, of course, even if you were up for a four-day road trip. In fact no one can drive to Juneau. You can fly in or hop a ferry, but not many people want to brave the frigid swells on the Inside passage waterways in January during the legislative session, so Juneau's always been known as the most inaccessible state capital in America. I wanted to change that too.

About a two-hour flight from Anchorage, Juneau sits at the base of Mount Juneau, enclosed by Auke Bay and hemmed in by dense forests. I think it's the nation's prettiest capital.

— — —

I also trimmed the state's food budget by keeping our home's freezer stocked with the world seafood we caught ourselves, as well as organic protein sources hunted by friends and family. We kept an interesting variety of food that way. If any vegans came over for dinner, I could whip them up a salad, then explain my philosophy on being a carnivore: *If God had not intended for us to eat animals, how come He made them out of meat?*

As Governor, though, hunting *was* an issue. I would face pressure from Hollywood to halt hunting, ban guns, and end our state's wildlife management practices, such as controlling predators. I said no to all of that nonsense: gun bans would destroy the Second Amendment, and as a life-long member of the NRA (Alaska has the highest NRA membership per capita in the nation), I had plenty of backup when telling Hollywood liberals what I thought of their asinine plans to ban guns. And we had to control predators, such as wolves, that were decimating the moose and caribou herds that feed our communities. People outside of Alaska are often clueless about our reliance on natural food sources. But as the ninety-year old Alaska Native leader Sydney Hunnington told Todd, "Nowadays, common sense is an endangered species."

— — —

Managing a $14 billion budget as the chief executive of the largest state in the Union with thousands of employees is more complex than managing a city like Wasilla, and certainly weightier than managing a household of seven.

But lessons learned on the micro level still apply to the macro. Just as my family couldn't fund every item on our wish list, and had to live within our means as well as save for the future, I felt we needed to do that for the state. I had four core principles as the foundation of our budget: live within our means, expand resource development and industry, focus on core services (education, infrastructure, and public safety), and save for the future. And I reminded my staff: never forget you're spending other people's money, that should make us more prudent and serious than anything.

Almost all of our state budget depends on development of Alaska's energy resources. The petroleum resource is non renewable. When it's gone, it's gone. Not only is it finite, its value fluctuates. In 1999, the price of a barrel of oil was $9; in 2008, it was $140. Price is dependent upon many factors — a war in a third world country, a hurricane off the coast, an angry petro-dictator, new oil discoveries in foreign lands. And our revenue department has to estimate every year what the price of a barrel of oil will be in order for us to build the budget.

Alaskan's know the pain of wildly fluctuating oil prices. We learned our lesson about saving for the future the hard way. During the heyday of the Trans-Alaska Pipeline, we were living the good life. The price of oil was high and the boom was on, creating a gold rush of state revenue, which government spent as quickly as possible. We were still a vast, undeveloped frontier outpost in need of infrastructure. So the state spent fast.

Then the smack-down: oil bottomed out at $9 a barrel. When the next boom came during my administration, we were determined to be conservative and accountable to future generations. (As Thomas Paine said in 1776: "If there must be trouble, let it be in my day, that my children may have peace.")

And so began our marathon budget breakdown. It was late June 2007, just after the solstice, and we worked late into the night with the warm midnight sun still pouring through my office windows.

— — —

My philosophy has always been that the most responsive and responsible level of government is the local level. Local government is best able to prioritize services and projects. That's the basis of the Tenth Amendment to the U.S. Constitution, which paraphrased, says that the powers not delegated specifically to the federal government or prohibited by the states are reserved to the states or the people themselves.

— — —

Ordinary Alaskans were expressing outrage at what was going on in Juneau, and I had promised to clean house. Remember the young political appointee who was supposed to be the ethics supervisor over IOGCC? In 2006, he was working as Governor Murkowski's chief legislative aide, representing the state in gasoline negotiations with ExxonMobile and other companies. A few months later, he was earning $10,000 a month lobbying the state for ExxonMobile. The public's obvious question: whose side are these guys on?

We were determined to keep the pressure on. That pressure paid off when legislators approved an omnibus ethics bill that imposed criminal penalties on lawmakers who traded votes for campaign contributions. Any legislator convicted of a felony would forfeit his state pension.

— — —

As with ethics reform, my team and I were determined to fundamentally change the game when it came to the natural gas pipeline. Instead of negotiating behind closed doors with the monopolistic industry, we wanted to get back to competitive free-market principles, ethically employed.

This was a multibillion-dollar project, the largest private-sector energy project in North American history. It was a once-in-a-lifetime opportunity. So we had to demand that the resource owners' needs be met. To get the project off the ground after decades of politicians just talking about it, we tried a "newfangled" approach: free market principles. We asked willing and able companies to compete for the right to build Alaska's gasline. Our approach would be open and transparent, with no behind-closed-door deals.

The project would cost the private sector a tremendous amount in government fees and prep work to get through local, state, and federal regulatory and environmental processes, so it made sense, along with the state's number of must-haves, for us to put some skin in the game by reimbursing the winning bidder for some of the up-front bureaucratic costs.

Therefore, in crafting what would become the landmark **Alaska Gasline Inducement Act**, or **AGIA**, we promised to reimburse up to $500 million in matching funds for the exclusive gasline license.

Still, Big Oil slammed us in the media — again, confirmation that we were making the right decisions. Soon after, we introduced AGIA to the legislature. That new word, "ah-gee-ah," quickly became part of the 49th State's vernacular. After much debate, the legislature adopted AGIA. In the end, only *one* lawmaker voted against the measure.

— — —

I discussed with representatives of other oil- and gas-producing states what America's needs are and how we can become energy-independent. I also assumed chairmanship of the **Interstate Oil and Gas Compact Commission (IOGCC)**, where I could help influence congress and the White House on energy and security issues.

— — —

"Go to hell, but resign first."
This particular crisp instruction was sent to DNR Commissioner Tom Irwin by a North Slope oil services company employee. **[(DNR) Department of Natural Resources]**
Irwin's recent actions had prompted the e-mail.
For the twenty-second time, ExxonMobile had submitted its plan to begin drilling in the Point Thomson Unit but still had not drilled. These domestic supplies of energy were needed. So with my full support, Tom had played hardball and took steps to prove that ExxonMobile was in default of its lease agreements.
My administration announced that for the state's and country's sake, ExxonMobile would no longer be allowed to just warehouse America's resources. After all these decades, if the largest company in the world wasn't going to

abide by its contracts to drill, we would rebid the leases and find a company that would.

That resulted in the kind note to Tom from an industry player about this employment future and eternal destination.

— — —

Adjacent to the much-discussed ANWR area, Point Thomson is a North Slope parcel of state-owned land that holds trillions of cubic feet of clean natural gas and an equally enormous amount of oil. The leases in question were the subject of a prior expansion agreement that would substantially enlarge the area in which ExxonMobile was permitted to drill. Of course, the big question was, why would DNR approve an expansion when ExxonMobile had sat on the unit for more than twenty-five years and had never successfully enlarged the area in which ExxonMobile had sat on the unit for more than twenty-five years and had never successfully sunk a drill bit?

— — —

When you deal with oil executives, you have to remember that they are used to winning. They also spend a lot of time in foreign countries dealing with leaders who carry pistols and whose bodyguards carry AK-47s. Meanwhile, the executives themselves are armed with bottomless bank accounts and highly trained platoons of fire-breathing lawyers. Thus reminding our friends in Big Oil that they have a contract that they're obligated to fulfill was really not going to scare them. A $20 million fine is "Pocket" change. But with their leases on the line — permanently — the question

ExxonMobile executives finally had to ask themselves was, do we really want to give up prime parcels that are loaded with billions of dollars' worth of natural resources that the public and our shareholders want us to develop? As AOGCC chair, when I wasn't butting heads with the state GOP, I was getting a thorough education in issues surrounding oil and gas recovery and production.

— — —

Two days after my first State of the State Address, I spoke to a group of energy explorers at an industry breakfast. It provided me with the perfect opportunity to set that stage and let our most powerful industry know how I would lead. Among the messages that I wished to send: Alaska is now open for business.

"You in the industry make your living by providing the goods and services necessary to get Alaska's resources to market," I said. "You live by contracts and legal obligations . . . Leases and unit agreements are contracts. Lessees must develop the public's resources or give back their leases."

ExxonMobile needed to develop now or let others compete to do so. In the larger scheme of things, I also knew that unless we accessed our known reserves on state lands, it would be more difficult to argue for access to federal lands such a ANWR. We had to prove we could do so safely and ethically before the Feds would let us develop in more controversial areas. As a state chief executive sitting across the table from well-heeled, lawyered-up executives, it was a given: you have to be committed to the position that is right for the people who hired you. You can't blink.

And we didn't.

Once we put our foot down, we won ruling after ruling after ruling. ... When you know you've made the right call, you stand your ground. DNR had made the right call. We would now see development.

Victory!

Two years into our term, Rolligons packed with drilling equipment started driving up the long ice road to Point Thomson to deploy hundreds of new workers in their hard hats and steel-toed boots. Exxon began ordering parts and supplies and buying equipment in order to develop rich resources for the industry, the state, and the nation. This was a bipartisan victory that created the mutually beneficial relationship between government and industry we had sought all along.

— — —

In the months following the AGIA vote, I was glad I'd trained for marathons. I'm superstitious about cutting any corners when I jog, believing the few extra steps can make a difference in the long race.

The competitive bidding process we created with AGIA unlocked the Big Three oil companies' development monopoly and threw open Alaska's doors to true competition and free enterprise. Suddenly, even other nations were bidding on the multibillion dollar project.

Early in 2008, the DNR and revenue commissioners finally announced their AGIA recommendation: the Calgary-based pipeline building giant TransCanada-Alaska, a firm that had not only met every single enforceable requirement of AGIA but exceeded them. We were ecstatic. *I* was ecstatic: there would be hundreds of steps yet to take, but we could almost envision the tape draped across the finish line.

— — —

On Friday, August 1, 2008, Alaskans won again: the legislature overwhelmingly voted to award the AGIA license to TransCanada-Alaska. We still had a long way to go until our clean, safe energy flowed south to the Lower 48, but after a thirty-year wait, we had turned the idea of commercializing our natural gas for Alaska's economic future from pipe *dream* to pipe*line.*

I had been elected governor of the state I loved. And in just the past year, we had kicked off the pipeline, overhauled ethics in state government, slashed state spending with my vetoes, saved for the future, and put money back into the hands of the people. Plus, we radically changed the way Alaskans would be secured in the futures with the natural resources they owned.

— — —

"Our Constitution demands that Alaskans come first. It will keep my compass pointed true north. It's the tool to build Alaska with strength and with order." I hit on the issues critical to our state: responsible energy resource development, cleaning up corruption, putting Alaskans to work in good jobs, reforming education, and nurturing that most precious resource — our children.

I emphasized my priorities of improving public safety and tackling substance abuse. Then I concluded with plain talk on the role of government, stressing fiscal restraint and the importance of competition and free enterprise. "Alaskans, hold me accountable, and right back at you!" I said.

"I'll expect a lot from you, too! Take responsibility for your family and for your futures. Don't think you need government to take care of all needs and to make your decisions for you. More government isn't the answer because you have ability, because you are Alaskans, and you live in a land that God, with incredible benevolence, decided to overwhelmingly bless."

We *were* shaking things up — and there'd be new energy for a new future.

— — —

My mission in office: to develop our state's resources in the best interests of the environment and of the people — including getting a gasline built. Ronald Reagan's principles: pick your departments and staff to implement your vision in other areas. Reagan concentrated on a few key issues and knocked them out of the park. That gave him the political capital to effect change in many other policy areas. I knew if I kept my campaign promise of overhauling the state in the areas of resource development, fiscal restraint, and ethical government, I would also be able to turn attention to equally urgent issues such as education, services for special needs and the elderly, job training, unemployment, and social ills in rural Alaska. We'd be able to do so with reprioritized funding to help the private sector provide opportunities in a way that would help Alaskans stand tall and independent.

— — —

We don't trust utopian promises from politicians. The role of government is not to perfect us but to protect us — to protect our inalienable rights. The role of government in a civil society is to protect the individual and to establish a social contract so the we can live together in peace.

— — —

Our prosperity has been driven by steady, abundant, affordable energy supplies. In Alaska, we understand the inherent link between energy and prosperity, energy and opportunity, and energy and security. I believe Alaska will lead the nation in developing both renewable and non renewable resources. I've always advocated an "all of the above" approach to energy production, and I support the harnessing of alternative sources of energy such as wind, solar, and geothermal. **Using renewable sources means developing nuclear energy, too.**

— — —

Some people ask whether we are still a republic, or whether we are becoming an empire, doomed to fade away like all the other empires once thought to be invincible.

We are still a republic. We are certainly not doomed to fade away. And we have no desire to be an empire. We don't want to colonize other countries or force our ideals on them. But we have been given a unique responsibility: to show the world the meaning and the rewards of freedom. America, as Reagan said, is "the abiding alternative to tyranny." We must remain the shining City on a Hill to all who seek freedom and prosperity.

— — —

But we must reawaken our belief in the principles that underlie our Constitution and the power we have when individuals stand together.

When we empower ourselves to stand up together, we become an even more blessed and prosperous nation. And we become a more generous nation, too — a nation that has proved for more than two centuries its willingness to share its blessings with others.`

Oil Beneath Our Feet

"I don't believe that God put us on earth to be ordinary"
— *Going Rogue, page 1*

Oil Beneath Our Feet

"There's no better training ground for politics than motherhood." — Going Rogue, p.115

Oil Beneath Our Feet

BORN AGAIN AMERICAN

WATCH THE VIDEO
http://tinyurl.com/bwnqtv

BORN AGAIN AMERICAN

I'm just a workin' man without a job,
It got shipped off to China, via Washington D.C.
And I know I'm nothin' special, there are plenty more like me,
but just the same,
I thought I knew the rules of the game

I stood up for this country that I love,
I came back from the desert, to a wife and kids to feed
I'm not sayin' Uncle Sam should give me what I need,
my offer stands,
I'll pull my weight 'you give me half a chance

And I went up to a congressman, and said to him, "You know
Our government is letting people down."
He said he'd need a lot of help to buck the status quo
I said there was a bunch of us around

I'm a Born, Again, American,
Conceived in liberty
My Bible and the Bill of Rights
My creed's equality
I'm a Born, Again, American
My country 'tis of me
And every-one who shares the dream
From sea to shining sea.

My brother's welding chassis at the plant
He's earning what our gran-dad did in nineteen forty-eight
While CEOs count bonuses behind the castle gates
How can they see, If all they care about's the do-re-me

It's getting where there's nowhere left to turn,
Not since the crash of twenty-nine have things been so unfair
So many of our citizens are living in despair,
The time has come, to reaffirm that hope's not just for some

The promise of America's surrendering to greed
The rule is just look out for number one,
But brace yourself 'cause some of us have sown a different seed,
A harvest of the spirit has begun.

II'm a Born, Again, American,
Conceived in liberty
My Bible and the Bill of Rights
My creed's equality
I'm a Born, Again, American
My country 'tis of me
And every-one who shares the dream
From sea to shining sea.

It's clear my country's soul is on the line,
She's hungering for something that she's lost along the way,
The principle the Framers called upon us to obey, That is this land,
The people's Will must have the upper hand

I felt the call, as once before, and took a sacred vow
And faithful to that vow I have remained,
I hear the call rhat once again my country needs me now
I hear her call I have been re-ordained

I'm a Born, Again, American,
Conceived in liberty
My Bible and the Bill of Rights
My creed's equality
I'm a Born, Again, American
My country 'tis of me
And every-one who shares the dream
From sea to shining sea.

And every-one who shares the dream,
From sea . . . to shining sea
America, . . America!

Oil Beneath Our Feet

"Gun bans will destroy the Second Amendment.
We have to destroy predators."
— Going Rogue, p.133

Oil Beneath Our Feet

"National leaders have a responsibility to respect the Tenth Amendment and keep their hands off the states. It's the old Jeffersonian view that the affairs of the citizens are best left in thier own hands." — Going Rogue, p.85

Lord Christopher Monckton
Third Viscount of Brenchley and Monckton

Breaking News

"Climategate" Debunked
Alex Jones / Christopher Monckton

"Climategate"

The still-developing scandal involving the release of thousands of e-mails and documents from a British climate research center.

The leaked documents expose some of the biggest political and scientific names in the global-warming debate to serious charges of fraud, unethical attacks on colleagues, censorship of opposing viewpoints, and possible criminal destruction of, and withholding of, scientific evidence.

Now the Climategate e-mails are showing that the corruption of science in the name or "saving the planet" from the supposed scourge of climate change is far more extensive and egregious than the public or the scientific community realized.

21

"Climategate" Debunked
Alex Jones / Christopher Monckton
Part One

BIG BROTHER. MAINSTREAM MEDIA. GOVERNMENT COVERUPS.

You want answers? Well, so does he. He's Alex Jones, on the GCN Radio Network.

And now, live from Austin, Texas . . . *Alex Jones.*

Alex Jones (AJ)

Thank you for joining us, for the first live broadcast of two-thousand and ten, the first live weekday transmission. We kicked it off yesterday, with the abbreviated Sunday, 4 to 6 PM, that I do every Sunday, because *we're in a war for Western Civilization. A war for liberty and freedom.*

Private offshore interests, the United Nations and others are openly setting up World Government.

Lord Christopher Monckton, of course, was the top Advisor to Margaret Thatcher. He has an international consulting firm on scientific and corporate issues to governments and fortune 500 [corporations]. He, of course, is an award winning journalist in his own right. His bio goes on and on. We'll give you his website several times before he leaves us today. He's with us graciously for the next hour.

He, with stunning accuracy . . . you know I don't say that for most guests unless it's warranted and due. But I want to single out his accuracy so that people can pay particular heed today with exactly the slogans, exactly the nomenclature, exactly what would happen at Copenhagen, how they would — even if it failed, — still have the bureaucracy try to implement it, which Gordon Brown has announced, treacherously, against the free Republics of the world.

And so he joins us to talk about what really happened at Copenhagen. What this new system is, by the industrialized world, saying, that they're going to monitor nation's carbon footprint, and go ahead and start levying the taxes and doling out Western taxpayer money from Europe, England, and the United States. And then we're going to move into the latest on Climategate and how these fraudsters are trying to take over at the local level.

Here in the United States taxes on TVs, at the state level in many states, taxes on plastic bags, home inspections. The UN has announced, with [Governor] Schwarzenegger, governors conferences, mayors conferences, doling out money for cities to implement this, circumventing the federal government, working with foreign powers. This is completely illegal and unconstitutional, and is an act of sedition.

So, we're going to break here in just a few minutes, and come back in a long segment.

But I want to introduce Lord Christopher Monckton.

Sir, great to have you here with us.

Lord Christopher Monckton (LM)

Well, Alex, its a real pleasure, once again, to be with you, and you're quite right, the usual suspects are still doing their best to, after the quite spectacular failure of the Copenhagen conference try and turn it into what in their terms is a success, by setting up what is called a high level panel, which is, if you like, a kind of **stub** of the world government they had hoped to grow. And they will hope to start transferring your money and mine to that high level panel along with the Copenhagen Green Fund. It's actually called the Copenhagen *Green* Fund. No longer any pretense of political objectivity. We're now in among the Reds who call themselves Green — the Watermelons — and they are now named as the *Green Fund* which is going to be the recipient of all this money that we're going to pay.

The United States, in particular, has said it's going to contribute really enormous sums of money, your money, to this *Green Fund,* and what its really going to be used for, of course, is not to help the poorer countries of the world adapt to climate change, because there's nothing to adapt to. It will be spent instead on setting up and growing the expensive, corrupt, central government bureaucracy of the new, very left-wing, virtually Marxist world government which the likes of Gordon Brown, and Obama, and Kevin Rudd in Australia, would so very much like to see, and which the countries like China and Russia, of course, who are also inclined in that authoritarian, totalitarian direction, are also inclined to follow.

So we haven't won as a result of Copenhagen . . . we certainly won on points but it is not yet a knockout. Much more work is to be done if we are to stop this very sinister movement towards undemocratic world government from carrying on any further.

Let us suppose that there *was* a scientific or economic case of doing anything about the climate.

AJ
We've got to break. Come right back.

Sorry to cut you off.

Third Viscount of Brenchley and Monckton, Lord Christopher Monckton, is our guest.

Please stay with us. We'll be right back as he gives us a worldwide briefing on what these criminals are up to.

— — —

AJ

If you had to single one person out as the General, or the George Washington of this fight against the climate criminals, the scaremongers who know it's a fraud, that want a tax to control all facets of life, it's Lord Christopher Monckton. He's the main Champion, the focal point, articulating the facts, predicting the enemy's movements and giving us the 'intell' to devastate their operations.

We've had a major victory at Copenhagen in this engagement, likening it to a naval engagement, but the enemy's main fleet is remassing to launch more attacks, circumnavigating the federal governments of the planet, going directly to the states, the counties, the cities.

Schwarzenegger leading that treacherous charge here, on the United States.

They're also having the bureaucracies of England, and the European Union, and the United States, ignore the people, and ignore . . . The UN wanted this treaty, wanted everybody to sign over their rights to world government and all these new taxes. They couldn't, so now they're creating the global fund, the *Green Fund,* to go buy-off governments, shut down their development. So Maurice Strong and others can suck more money out, like they did with the 'Oil for Food' program.

22
"Climategate" Debunked
Alex Jones / Christopher Monckton
Part Two

AJ

So, Sir, break down what really happened at Copenhagen. The Dragon is wounded, but not yet slain. Then get into the Climategate investigation . . . The criminal investigations that have been initiated in different parts of the globe.

Sir, you have the floor. Thank you for joining us to brief our listeners

LM

Well, Alex. I'm going to continue with your military metaphor. I'm going to take a kind of three minute time-out, because I'm going to recite to you, now, an address which was given by Abraham Lincoln in a reedy voice, holding the paper very closed to his face, on the battlefield of Gettysburg. This is what he said . . .

Four score and seven years ago our fathers brought forth on this continent, a new nation, conceived in Liberty, and dedicated to the proposition that all men are created equal.

Now we are engaged in a great civil war, testing whether that nation, or any nation so conceived and so dedicated, can long endure. We are met on a great battlefield of that war. We have come to dedicate a portion of that field, as a final resting place for those who here gave their lives that that nation might live. It is altogether fitting and proper that we should do this.

But, in a larger sense, we cannot dedicate — we cannot consecrate — we cannot hallow — this ground. The brave men, living and dead, who struggled here, have consecrated it, far above our poor power to add or detract. The world will little note, nor long remember what we say here, but it can never forget what they did here. It is for us the living, rather, to be dedicated here to the unfinished work which they who fought here have thus far so nobly advanced. It is rather for us to be here dedicated to the great task remaining before us — that from these honored dead we take increased devotion to that cause for which they gave the last full measure of devotion — that we here highly resolve that these dead shall not have died in vain — that this nation, under God, shall have a new birth of freedom — and that government of the people, by the people, for the people, shall not perish from the earth.

Now that's what he said. And that's what I want to talk about now, because let us suppose that there *is* a case for doing something about the climate — there *isn't* but let's pretend there is.

Let us suppose that even if there isn't a scientific case, there is an economic case, — there isn't but let's pretend there is. If we're going to have multilateral action, if we're going to have a global government, then honoring what it was those gallant men at Gettysburg died for, we want to make sure that that government shall be a government of the people, by the people, and for the people. It should be an *elected* government.

What I would like everyone who is listening today to do is to get in touch by telephone with their elected Representatives, both in Congress, and both your Senators, and say that if we are to go any further whatsoever toward paying taxpayers' money toward this high level panel of the Copenhagen *Green Fund,* these first steps toward what would have been a much grander world government unless we had stopped it at Copenhagen, but it may still come to that, we want to make sure that if there's going to be a world government, it should be an *elected* world government, elected by the people of the world, and not *appointed* by the bureaucrats of the world, as is at present intended.

That is a sensible point.

We're saying if there *was* a problem with the climate — which of course there isn't — if there is an economic solution to it — which you and I don't believe there is — if we must have a global government — which you and I don't believe we must have — then I'm sure that everybody who is a true American and a follower of Lincoln, will admit that that is to be an *elected* government, and not an appointed one.

We have to stop this step-by-step, crab-wise approach towards the global government which is what they are now going to try to do, because so many of your listeners, Alex, got on to their Senator's before and said the Treaty of Copenhagen, in it's original draft which I warned you about shall not pass. We will not have it.

So many of you actually did that. But the democratic Senators, in particular, got in touch with President Obama and said, We can't *have* this. We're *not* having this, We'll *never* get it through. We'll *never* be voted for again if we throw away the democracy for which our people at Gettysburg died, and for which our people are still dying for it.

Our gallant troops now, yours and ours, in Afghanistan and in Iraq. These lives must not be thrown away in vain. Government of the people, by the people, for the people . . . that is what the United States is all about, and any administration that tries to transfer power away from the Congress that you the people elect, towards some alien, bureaucratic, senseless, dismal dictatorship somewhere else, is as you have rightfully said, committing high treason, and should be flung from office and impeached.

Am I putting this too strongly to you?

AJ

No Sir. And I've noticed you have a great knowledge of our system of government here.

When you have Gordon Brown saying I don't care if the nations didn't sign on to this, I'm setting up this fund and we'll now have Europe, the UK, and the United States and Canada, New Zeland, Australia and others, he calls them the Commonwealths — sign on to this and start putting money into what he and others have called global government, that is open tyranny.

And to have Schwarzenegger all over the news saying, well I'm just going to have a governor's conference meet that he's calling himself, and I'm going to have a group of mayors meet, and we're going to implement this taxing system even if the Senate won't, and a week before Copenhagen ended you said they may not get this through, but they are still going to try to implement it through the bureaucracy and through the local governments. Is this not glaring sedition to have some usurping, foreign born governor running around organizing the states, and then to have Obama, who can't get the Senate to pass it, it looks like, just saying he'll take money from the treasury and serve it up to Ban Ki Moon and Maurice Strong. It's just outrageously, openly, fraudulent and criminal.

LM

Well, certainly under *our* constitution, such as it is, and we don't have a written one like you, no money can be handed away by the government to anyone unless Parliament has authorized it. Now the trouble is, at the moment, our Parliament is a lot of 'poodles' and they, on all three parties, believe in this climate nonsense, and if Gordon Brown says to them, never mind that our own people are starving and going bust at a record rate, we must give their money away "to save the planet" from this non-problem of the climate. Unfortunately, I think it's quite likely that in any budget act, our Parliament would probably be like a poodle and just vote for it . . . at the moment . . . because reality has not yet broken through among our governing class here. Now in the United States I'm less familiar with exactly what powers the president has under his executive authority to allocate money from the treasury or the fed to whatever project he fancies, but I think I'm right is saying . . .

AJ

Sir, it's totally illegal. He can't do it. And Congress is already saying that.

Eighteen Attorney Generals are saying they may file suit, and its not just that, it's healthcare, everything he's doing is unconstitutional.

LM

I think that often happens on the left these days.

They . . . he knows . . . Obama knows, from his plummeting rates in the opinion polls, that he's not long for this world. He will be a lame duck President from this December, once the mid-term election for the entire House of Representatives has been held. He knows this now. And so, in panic, he's trying to do what the left *always* does, pay no attention to the Constitution, use taxpayer money to fund his friends, and setup various bureaucracies that will go on repeating the extreme left, Marxist point of view, even once he has deservedly been flung out of office.

If you have as many as eighteen Attorney Generals willing to file suit, and say, Just a moment, you can't spend taxpayer's money without the authorization of Congress, then even Obama's 'poodles' on the Supreme Court, which at the moment seems to be the weakest part of your Constitution, because it's not upholding the Constitution the way that it should, I don't think even *they* can go along with Obama's antics.

23
"Climategate" Debunked
Alex Jones / Christopher Monckton
Part Three

AJ

Our guest's website is *scienceandpublicpolicy.org*
Lord Christopher Monckton is our guest.

We've had a giant victory, and we can feel the momentum shifting in our direction, but still, the hundreds of billions globally invested in the fraud, in the global government, in the taxation scheme, as the foundation of this illegal unelected global government, they're not going to stop, they're going to keep pushing, though badly damaged. So it is up to the people to contact their Senator, their Representatives, their state leaders, and say no, no, no.

Please continue Lord Monckton.

LM

What you need to say, now, when you talk to your Representatives. Say that if there must be **any** kind of global government, it must be **elected by the people of the world,** and not appointed by the government or by the bureaucrats. **Its' got to be elected.** And that will stop the nonsense gaster than anything.

So now . . . on to the latest on Climategate . . .

I've now heard from the Chairman of the independent inquiry into Climategate, because I wrote to him and said, I want to give evidence of this. He said that he's about to appoint a team to look at who's going to give evidence and who is not, and at that point they'll get back to me, and so that is slowly happening.

More interestingly, arising out of Climategate, there is now a general mood in the air that those who have been peddling this climate scare for so long, and who have quite wrongly claimed the moral high ground, are now losing it, not only because the science doesn't work out, not only because there is no economic advantage, even if the science did work out, not only because even if we had to have something to do economically even with it, we don't need a global government to do it. Not even if we **do** have a global government, it must be an **elected** government.

The reason why they've lost the moral authority, above all else, is that it is becoming apparent that you are quite right, Alex, when you use words like 'criminal,' and 'fraud,' about what's going on.

For instance, the Chairman of the IPCC Science Panel, Dr. Rajenda Pachaurie. When I was in Copenhagen, I went to hear him give a lecture, on why it is that the climate is all terrible, and we've got to do something about it, and I knew that he would use, and he duly did use a bogus graph that appeared three times as large, and in full color, in the latest UN document published in 2005 about the climate, an entirely bogus graph which was created, using a false and well known false and fraudulent statistical technique, and tried to pretend, quite falsely, that the rate of warming is itself *increasing,* and I confronted him, as he arrived at that lecture, and handed him a detailed letter from me explaining what was wrong that graph, telling him *not* to use it, and asking him to get back to me within 48 hours to say that that graph would no longer be used either by him of my the ITCC. And that this kind of fraud would, in the future, would be desisted from. I also raised a question at the end of his speech, having seen him *use* the graph, saying, look, you've used it again and this is a bogus graph, and I'm going to five you 48 hours to get back to me. He didn't get back to me in 48 hours of course, and I am now reporting him to the police in India for scientific and financial fraud, because he has a large financial, vested interest in numerous corporations, and is making money out of this climate scare.

AJ

You were saying a year ago that he was involved. It's firmly all over British and U.S. papers that they're shutting down famous steel plants in England to open them up in India where he's one of the big owners.

LM

That's right, and he's making money out of that. We've lost 1700 jobs in the North of England just in the last month as a result of the closure of a major steel work at Red Car that has now been transferred to India where they're going to build exactly the same steel work, and they're going to be making money twice, first of all because they get money from us because we're no longer doing the carbon emissions, and second, because by using our steel works and its technology, they will be emitting less carbon that they would have been by any other method of steel production, and we are paying at both ends for this, and our workers are loosing their jobs.

AJ

Outrageous! The British are **paying** for loosing their jobs.

LM

That's right. We are paying per salary, personally, to take 1,700 of our workers jobs and transfer — not the workers, just the jobs — to India where he will make money again by various credits under the clean development mechanism which is just another boondoggle run by the United Nations.

It's unbelievable!

24

"Climategate" Debunked
Alex Jones / Christopher Monckton
Part Four

AJ

The leading voice against the foundation of world government, *the Climate Cult,* which Al Gore admits will be a *New Religion.* [Ed. reminiscent of Dark Age Priests selling **"Indulgences"** (licenses) to Church-goers *for the forgiveness of sins,* both *before* and after Church-goers commited the sins. By sin was many a Cathedral built.]

If you want to understand these people and see the UN's own documents, their own statements, understand what they will set up, if successful, a total ecological tyranny, of collectivism, transferring our money to those criminal bureaucracies, you need to get my film **Endgame: Blueprint For Global Enslavement.** You can get this film free for a limited time with **Fall Of The Republic: The Presidency Of Barack H. Obama,** detailing the climate scam, the fraudsters, how they're running the scam, what they plan to do with it, how to beat them, — at *inforwars.com.*

We were getting into fraud and the Head of the IPCC openly profiting, with Gordon Brown paying taxpayer money to shut down high quality jobs that have been there for a long time, to ship them for his profit. Then there is the classic Climategate e-mails where Ben Santer admits that he *removed* five section from the UN's IPCC Report on Man-made Global Warming, where their own scientists said Man wasn't doing it, and perhaps we should revisit that, and *more* of where climate is right now.

Lord Monckton:

LM

Let's finish off on Dr. Pachauri. The other thing I've done is to report him to the British Charity Commission with a request that they should pass on the details to the police, because he runs . . . along with Christian Dekel and Sir John Horton, who is the former Chairman of the IPCC . . . a Charity called TERI EUROPE founded originally by TATAR STEEL, and of course, it's TATAR STEEL which happens to be taking over this steel works, shutting it down in the UK and opening it in India to make more profit twice over out of our subsidies and destroying 1,700 of our jobs.

Well this man Pachauri, because these jobs are being destroyed . . . I'm now having a very close look at him and what he's doing to our people, and I discovered that he set up this charity along with the former Chairman of the IPCC, the UN Climate Panel, John Horton, and that charity, in each of the last 3 years, have declared income of only 7 or 8,000 sterling, in fact, in the last 4 years added together, less than 25,000 sterling, and yet on the website of the government Department of the Environment, here, I found a grant of 30,714 lbs just in one year, 2006-2007 to the TATAR ENERGY RESEARCH INSTITUTION in Europe. This Charity which has declared only 25,000 lbs of income total over 4 years on one grant on one of its projects, it has received more than the money it declared for four years.

Now that is false accounting, and I have asked for an explanation from the Commission and information. There may be, and lets be fair, an innocent explanation, but I'm a bloat if I can *see* one.

And what I think is building up here is a sense that these people thought that they have become above the law.

They thought they had got the mainstream media where they wanted them, that nobody would ask any questions about any of this, that they could do what they like, with British people's jobs, and other people's jobs. There's just been a large American aluminum smelter closed down, again about 2,500 jobs destroyed overnight.

Why? Because the company that ran it can no longer find anyone to sell it electricity to run the smelter, because those aluminum smelters take a lot of electricity, and because the Green-Ears and environmental Marxists have gone around banning the building of new coal fired power stations, and also stopping nuclear ones being built, America is running out of nuclear energy that is needed to safeguard jobs. Its happening in America, major closes, it's happening in Britain, major closes, major losses of jobs directly attributed to the financial and scientific fraud, for that is what it now is, and we're now getting at a number of different places . . . we're now getting investigations.

There is, of course, now, the Climategate investigation.

Now, the original items of reference were rather soft, it was just a bit of a slap on the wrist for the university for having to have not complied with the freedom of information act when other scientists asked for information. That's bad enough, heaven knows, in a matter where they're about to spend trillion on the say-so of these scientists that we cannot check because they won't give us their data, but on top of that, I have *now* written to the chairman of the inquiry who has been appointed, and I said, look, there is a large scientific and financial fraud underlying all this and since I am named in these Climatgate e-mails, because they don't like me very much, and you can imaging the nasty scientists who are trying to under-mine the world with their bogus science.

I said, since they have named me in uncomplimentary terms in the e-mails, I want the right of reply by having the right to explain to the Inquiry why I say that it is a financial and scientific fraud, and I'm going to produce all the evidence I've built up of all these particular people who are named in the Climategate e-mails as writing to each other in furtherance of this report.

I'm going to show what they have done, over the years.

I gave a presentation of this in Copenhagen, and you should have seen the jaws dropping all around the room, and I said I've been following all these people for years. I've been watching them committing scientific fraud. I suspected all along that they were linked, and now we have the evidence, thanks to the Climategate whistle blower, showing that they are linked.

This is an organized conspiracy of *not* very many people. It's not as if we were talking of thousands of scientists in this conspiracy. It's about **two dozen.** They have effectively driven the whole show by being absolutely *vicious* to any scientist who dared to disagree with them. They've had scientists sacked from their jobs, they've had them threatened, they've had them bullied, they've denied them access to the peer review Journals, they've stopped them from getting their material into the UN Climate Report.

These people have been *driving* this scare and they have been so nasty that they've *terrified* ordinary scientists who are not very political and who aren't very strong willed, into silence so that they could then claim that because none of these other scientists dare to argue with them, for fear of losing their jobs, there is therefore a consensus. That is the nastiest kind of fraud.

25
"Climategate" Debunked
Alex Jones / Christopher Monckton
Part Five

AJ

Lord Monckton. Then when they . . . 31,000 scientists . . . did try to testify last year in Congress, they were blocked from being able to testify, even though they've been persecuted. But expanding on that, I saw a number in the BBC just a month ago of China opening a new coal-powered plant every *2-1/2 days!* And right here in East Texas I have some family-land and family that lives there. They were going to build a new clean burning coal plant to power several new factories that were going to be coming in and none of that happened because local environmentalists, under Green funding from the UN and federal government, ran around terrorizing, and threatening law suits, and it didn't happen, and so those plants were not built anywhere in the United States.

It was multiple, clean burning coal-powered pants that literally nothing comes out of there but steam and carbon dioxide. And we see Al Gore, and we see the government, we see Maurice Strong, we see George Soros. They control . . . and you've spoken about this but if you can elaborate briefly, about how they get to decide where the federal money goes for new energy, and its always invested with *their* companies that they make profits from.

I mean this isn't just them trying to set up a global government and tax system, it's a New Dark Age where they're

America's Energy Non-Crisis!   197

the only people who get a letter of marque or license from this new imperial Crown of the UN to be able to even engage in any type of manufacturing.

LM

Of course. What is egregiously *terrifying* about this, is that you quite rightly laid stress on the fact that 157 coal fired plants throughout the United States, are now on hold because of the environmental activism of the nastiest kind. Exactly as you say, the same threats and bullying which the scientists are doing to each other, are being done by the environmentalists to the coal corporations and to the businesses that want to set up factories or run their Aluminum smelters.

These people are saying that you can't build these coal fired plants, here, so what's happening is, China is building them over in China. How do we know? Because the Chinese administration publish it every year in what is called the Annual Statistical Communique of the People of the Republic of China, and in that communique, they said that they were going to *continue* regardless of what the UN said and they were going to build one or two coal fired power plants *every week,* for the foreseeable future. Every week! It means that in one year they will have built almost as many coal fired plants as the environmentalists have stopped being built in the United States in the last 10 years, and those are *dirty, dirty* plants using dirty coal with huge pollutants . . . The Asian brown hay is the only artifact of man that can be see from space during the day.

The coal is burnt in a dirty way which pollutes the atmosphere in a way that it doesn't in the United States.

All of this has nothing to do with the environment. You

should understand that. It has nothing whatever to do with the environment. It is only to do with power politics and the goal of these power politics is to dismantle the West, to dismantle the United states, to leave you and us enfeebled and incapable, so that a few very rich men and very rich corporations — people like Al Gore who doesn't deserve to be rich.

They are the people who are profiteering out of the lies that they are spreading and you must help to . . . if you find them telling lies, complain to the police. The police are beginning to take an interest in this fraud, now.

Complain to the police if you think you're being lied to. Just go into your local police station and say, I've had enough of this, look what it's costing in jobs and in money and in taxation. Complain to the police and make them investigate. They have a duty to investigate fraud. And fraud is what this is. It's a biggest fraud that has ever been perpetrated on the world, and you must fight it, or you will go under.

AJ

Is this not economic espionage where Maurice Strong, the Rockefellers and others openly are the bigger investors in China. They're all making money, there are no law standards and they're trying to deindustrialize the US, as Maurice Strong has stated. They're doing this to England, they're doing this to Europe, making Europe completely dependent on Russia for natural gas.

I mean this is just . . . the more you look at this crime, it's so diabolical, its so multifaceted, It is so incredibly evil. How do we stop this fraud?

LM

I think that what you do is do exactly what you're doing now. You tell the people of the United States that it is happening and in the end they won't tolerate it.

Let me give you just one example, picking up on your point there, about the natural gas.

Now *every day* in the North Slope of Alaska where there is an oil field, they flare off enough natural gas to supply the whole of Western Europe. Now if it were not for the . . . again the environmentalists who have stopped that gas pipeline from being built from the North Slope down to the ice free ports of South Alaska . . . across Alaska . . . if that pipeline had been allowed then I could send 4 large super-tankers *every day* to Anchorage [Valdez] lets say, pick-up the gas from there, sail it to Greensmouth, plug it into the European gas network, there, and I could supply the whole of Europe on gas which at the moment is being burned into the atmosphere creating enormous amounts of CO_2 — which is what they say they are worried about — from the North Slope of Alaska.

That is how *mad* all of this is. It is not just that it is *bad* . . . of which it is . . . and all these people making fortunes. There's the Rothschilds. Rothschild, for instance, he's just opened a huge gold mine in Russia and is making millions, millions, millions out of it, and they're all doing it in some ways . . . good luck to them, its good that they're making money . . . but what they are also doing is using their financial power to lobby against innocent businesses in the

US — such as that Aluminum smelter — such as all these coal fired power plants, and nuclear power stations that are so necessary — lobbying against the building of the gas pipeline that could liberate Europe from Russian gas, and keep us with our independence, and get our gas from what is now simply being wasted into the atmosphere in Alaska.

Oil Beneath Our Feet

"Climategate" Debunked
Alex Jones / Christopher Monckton
Part Six

AJ

This is Monopoly Capitalism. If the pendulum is swinging against these people and the public is now beginning to learn some of the magnitude, not even the *full* magnitude of the fraud, where do we go from here?

CM

Right. I think the next step is this. The first thing the UN is going to try . . . I would if I were in its shoes . . . is to bring forward the next annual Conference of the states parties Convention on Climate Change which is due to be held in Mexico next December to pick up from what Copenhagen did. They may try to bring that forward to June because they don't want to find after the next mid-term election in the US that they can no longer get any legislation on their side through either House of the Congress.

And that's what will happen, I think, after the next mid-term election, because people *do* listen to your program, Alex, they listen to the other program that I talk on quite regularly, and they are getting the *message* . . . that they are *now* governed by people who really, seriously mean them harm!

And I'm sorry to, if you like, intervene in your politics as a Brit' . . . and if there are any supporters of President

Obama listening to this, then I do apologize for having to say this . . . but he is now a *danger* to the United States of America . . . and in particular . . . a *danger* to the working people of the United States of America, because they're the people . . . it's the people who run the aluminum smelters, the people who would be digging the coal that now can't be dug, and who would be running the power stations that can't be built, who would be working in those factories in Texas, that you mentioned that can't be built, that would have been driven by the power stations that can't be built.

These are the people . . . the working people who are gradually . . . by a 1,000 here, or 2,000 there . . . losing their jobs with no hope of getting their jobs back because the industries in which they once worked, or might have worked, will never arrive again. Because you have an administration that is *determined to shut America down!*

AJ

Well, Lord Monckton . . . this is a global threat we face, as you said, calling for a **world-freedom-** or a **world-liberty-party** based in each sovereign nation. We are facing a global threat. Its' good that I can warn people in England. And you can warn people here in America.

We're facing the same threat, so we know what we're dealing with here.

LM

That's right. This is a global threat. And you're right to remind people it's not just in the United States, it's not just *Obama.* We've got Kenneth Rudd in Australia who after he heard my MN speech — in which I first drew attention to the world government provisions in the Copenhagen Treaty

— he devolved an entire speech of 3/4 hour to personally vilifying me and he was really angry that this plot to set up a world government had been exposed, so he needs to be dealt with, and I'm going to Australia in 2 weeks time to do a tour of all Australia to let people hear this side of the story that the mainstream media simply won't tell them.

And let me tell you what's happening down there in Australia this moment.

The government . . . and it was the previous administration, so again I'm not making political points here. The previous administration did a deal with the UN by which to comply with the Kyoto Protocol and cut their carbon emissions. They said if we designate the farmland of half of Australia as being a *carbon sink* that can't be farmed, that will allow us to comply with our obligation under the Kyoto Protocol. And the UN for some reason said yes to the protocol. Then it means that the people who own thousands of acres of farmland are now suddenly not allowed to farm it, and there's been no compensation at all. So it's not only in America that terrible things are happening, and people are losing their livelihood, and of course, their financial asset in their farmland. Because its worthless now because nobody can do anything with it, it's got to be left fallow.

And one poor farmer who has been heart-broken by this sudden, unexpected loss of his livelihood and of the capital loss of his farm, without a penny of compensation from the Australian government, in the name of complying with this *ludicrous Kyoto Protocol,* has climbed up a Television mast on his estate — he's living half way up it now with water only — he's been on a hunger strike now for six long weeks, 42 days, and I fear he's not long for this world, but he's so *angry* about what is happening to him . . . and yet not one of the mainstream news media has even reported that this is what's being done to farmers all across Australia.

The silence of the mainstream media is culpable and *serious* and something is going to have to be done about it.

"Climategate" Debunked
Alex Jones / Christopher Monckton
Part Seven

AJ

Well that's obviously because they're very, very scared of the truth, and have seen reports in Australian news in the last two years in a *positive* way saying, isn't it great . . . this farmer will not be paid . . . and no more sheep . . . or no more corn . . . and they just calmly announce it.

And here in the US they're talking about taking the land off-use. And the Supreme Court ruled in **New London vs. Kelo** that they can take your property *without just compensation.* I mean *this is the heart of tyranny* . . . not just taking property, and the power to tax, and power to destroy, and taxation without representation . . . but *now* we'll just take your factories. We'll give $25 billion to the automakers, as a bailout, so they can move to Russia, move to Eastern Europe, move to Brazil, move to China, and they're **paying** to move jobs, They're **paying** to shut down farms and factories, because we're bankrupt, we'll be fully dependent upon the globalists.

That is their plan, and you know as well as I do, Lord Monckton, the UN has stated this in their Biological Diversity Assessments. Maurice Strong has said this is just a group wanting to visit **feudalism,** and **serfdom** upon the planet so they can play *God,* and its just so outrageous to witness this unfolding!

LM

And now listeners, when you have heard what Alex has just said, you might have thought this too extreme. Its just silly.

The trouble is, this is actually happening. The stories we are telling you are *real*. Factories being closed down, big ones, in Britain. Factories being closed here in the United States that would have opened, not opening. In Australia, farmland being taken out of use. And now a *new* and pernicious *extension* of the doctrine of Eminent Domain. Not only can the state take away your land in the United States, they can take it away without a penny of compensation, as it's already being done in Australia.

And all of this in the name of a problem that doesn't exist. **There is no climate problem.** The climate has *always* changed, it always *will,* humankind has a *minuscule* effect at the very worst. We are a bit-part player in all of this.

There is no danger. We could burn as much fossil fuel as we like, create as much CO_2 as we like. It wouldn't make any difference to the climate.

But these people have managed, by lying and lying, and lying again, to *pretend* that there is a problem where there isn't one. And who's going to get hurt the most? It's not the *rich.* It's not the *big boys.* It's the working class. The people who voted, in the millions, for President Obama, who voted, in the millions, for Kevin Rudd, in Australia, who voted for Gordon Brown. It's the working people.

AJ

And we know at its heart it's all about population control

to limit our numbers, and that's why the UN says they want to shut off the food to the third world. You pointed out, this is a death sentence to the third world where they are going to implement that, and, in closing, obviously its circumstantial. They always use hot weather, which is really *normal,* in certain bio-sphere areas, as to say, look its *hot* look, Oh look, there's a *dust storm.*

Certainly if they would have chosen global cooling as their fear mongering they would be using the news now that we see. Massive deaths in India from record cold. Record cold in D.C. Record snowfall in areas of Europe. Record cold in the last 100 years around the globe, because the satellites and ground data show cooling for nine years levelling out in the last ten. Correct?

LM

That's exactly right. The last 15 years there's been no significant warming, and this winter there is likely to be one of the coldest six winters of the whole of the last 100 years. Now of course, one bad winter doesn't make a trend, but we have now had *three* bad winters, on the trot, in the Northern Hemisphere.

We've had three bad *summers,* on the trot, certainly in the United Kingdom. So certainly, we're not getting the pattern of relentless, rapid warming which is what the models predicted. But of course, again, they will say that a short trend is not necessarily a long trend, and you can get down-trends even in an up-rend.

Yes you can, but it's now becoming apparent that over the last 30 years we simply haven't seen anything like the warming that the models have predicted. They have got it wrong, exactly as we said they had, and there's now no one denying it, and yet they are cruelly killing off the jobs of working people throughout the Western World, and all of this for chimera, all of this to make themselves rich at your expense.

AJ

And of course, they *also* sell it as if they want to help the third world, but by their own admission this would kill tens of millions a year of those who are on the verge of starvation.

LM

It already is killing tens of millions. The awful thing is the doubling of world food prices, that was called by the biofuel scam taking 1/3rd of the US agricultural land out of producing food for people who needs it, to producing fuel for the klunkers who don't.

The effect of that has doubled world food prices, pricing food out, so that poor people around the world can't afford it. There have been major food riots in a dozen different regions. People are being killed world wide by the false belief in global warming that is so fake and so bogus. These profiteers are profiting out of the death of millions in poorer countries . . . and not a word of this is appearing in any of our mainstream newspapers!

AJ

Isn't that . . . Lord Monckton . . . genocide under the Nurenberg Code?

LM

Yes, I think you make a very good point there, and I

think that if somebody were to bring Al Gore up in front of the International Criminal Court for having caused the death of millions by the lies that he has been spreading, a conviction would be found. He would be found guilty of crimes against humanity, and the penalty for those, that various people have discovered recently . . . is death!

AJ

Lord Christopher Monckton, our guest from the United Kingdom.

References

1. http://tinyurl.com/ycynpq2

2. http://tinyurl.com/y9r9yrg

3. http://tinyurl.com/ybz2cyd

4. http://tinyurl.com/yer4ejb

5. http://tinyurl.com/yazctkw

6. http://tinyurl.com/ycos77b

7. http://tinyurl.com/ybr5wug

Oil Beneath Our Feet

"My God shall supply all your need according to his riches in glory by Christ Jesus." — *Phillipians 4:19*

Oil Beneath Our Feet

"If my people, which are called by my name, shall humble themselves, and pray, and seek my face, and turn from their wicked ways; then I will hear from heaven, and will forgive their sin, and will heal their land."

— 2 Chronicles 7:14

"'For I know the plans that I have for you,' declares the Lord. 'Plans for peace and not for calamity, to give you a future and a hope. When you call upon Me I will hear you, when you search for me you will find Me; if you seek Me with all your heart.'" — Jeremiah 29:11-13, Going Rogue, p.103

Oil Beneath Our Feet

*"Are we really grateful for the good already received?
Then we shall avail ourselves of the blessings we have,
and thus be fitted to receive more."*

*Science and Health with Key to the Scriptures,
by Mary Baker Eddy,* page 3:22-24

Oil Beneath Our Feet

Commercial Redemption: The Hidden Truth
http://tinyurl.com/yj4otn4

Untold History Of America: Let The Truth Be Told
http://tinyurl.com/y8hwvzr

*New Beginning Study Course: Connect The Dots
And See*
http://tinyurl.com/yc4jkyd

Monitions of a Mountain Man: Manna, Money, & Me
http://tinyurl.com/ygtkak8

Maine Street Miracle: Saving Yourself And America
http://tinyurl.com/ybss3ss

*Reclaim Your Sovereignty: Take Back Your Christian
Name*
http://tinyurl.com/ydx92ev

*Epistle to the Americans I: What you don't know
about The Income Tax*
http://tinyurl.com/yfplutf

*Epistle to the Americans II: What you don't know
about American History*
http://tinyurl.com/yzme458

*Epistle to the Americans III: What you don't know
about Money*
http://tinyurl.com/yzuffbe

America's Energy Non-Crisis!   221

www.ingramcontent.com/pod-product-compliance
Lightning Source LLC
Chambersburg PA
CBHW062142280526
45788CB00001B/270